Advance Praise for *Still, in the City*

"*Still, in The City* is an amazing collection of *Dharma* practice stories, narratives of the messiness of the present moment and opening to freedom of heart and mind right there in the midst of it. They are lessons learned about how mindfulness practice is both the same and yet different because of where it is practiced; not better, but different. Each author inspires with their willingness to keep trying no matter the confusion they initially face; their willingness to keep working with things long enough to enable wisdom to arise is the gift they offer to the reader."

—Sharon Salzberg, author of *Lovingkindness:*
The Revolutionary Art of Happiness

"Mindfulness and Compassion practice in daily life? *Still, in the City* has many thoughtful and inspiring essays by *Dharma* practitioners and teachers, all ways to bring the teachings alive just where you are."

—Jack Kornfield, author of *A Path with Heart*

"This is a book for those whose spiritual practice lives in the fierce light of day. As a New Yorker, a collection of authentic, personal expressions like these are critical. They are stories of unflinching intimacy that expand the temple, meditation hall, and *sangha* to the streets, subway cars, and communities of our predominantly urban lives. The heart of this book moves with the hearts of all beings, conveying a sacred dignity in our everyday circumstances and struggles. *Still, in the City* is as critical for beginners interested in exploring mindfulness practice as it is for those devoted to the justice, equity, and love of a fully expressed Buddhadharma."

—Greg Snyder, Senior Director &
Associate Professor of Buddhist Studies,
Union Theological Seminary, Dharma Teacher &
Senior Priest, Brooklyn Zen Center

"*Still, in the City* is an insightful collection of practical wisdom bathed in the heart of the *dharma*. These seasoned practitioners invite us into deeper presence, understanding, and intimacy with the simplicity and complexity of our day-to-day lives, regardless of our surroundings or circumstances. We need this book to better understand our lives and our belonging. A must read and must share offering that reveals the healing power of wise awareness."

—Ruth King, author of *Mindful of Race:
Transforming Racism from the Inside Out*

"This book could be titled 'Buddhism Made Real' because the authors describe their firsthand experience of practicing Buddhism in the fullness and the complexity of modern life. The book is inspiring and heartwarming."

—Gil Fronsdal, co-teacher at the Insight Meditation
Center in Redwood City, California and
Insight Retreat Center in Santa Cruz, California

"*Still, in the City* is a perfect book for the modern Buddhist reader. Underpinned with deep *dharma*, it presents engaging tools for living in the realm of *samsara* from a wise, compassionate, and diverse group of teachers and senior practitioners. Taking wisdom to the streets, they help keep these ancient teachings alive in our troubled world."

—Kevin Griffin, author of
One Breath at a Time: Buddhism and the Twelve Steps
and *Living Kindness: Buddhist Teachings for a Troubled World*

"I am so excited about [this] book. What you are offering here will be a great refuge to urban meditators. At one point in my own practice I asked myself, 'What are you doing here? Are you seeking to quiet the storm? Or are you trying to find the quiet within the storm?' Until I posed that question I hadn't given full weight to the power of the inner quiet. When we can develop that, we can manage the storm. To me [this] book establishes an apt metaphor for finding that quiet within the storm. We can't make everyone else bow to our wishes for stillness. But we don't need to. The inner quiet is much more accessible and practical anyway. So good on you for helping that along! Congratulations!"

—Gloria Taraniya, Ambrosia,
Barre Center for Buddhist Studies

"Both practical and poetic, *Still, in the City* provides enormously helpful advice on how to undertake serious *dharma* practice where the vast majority of us *actually* live. This is a beautiful, rich anthology that fills a critical gap in the literature."

—Sumi Loundon Kim, Yale University,
author of *Sitting Together: A Family-Centered Curriculum
on Mindfulness, Meditation, and Buddhist Teachings*

STILL,
IN THE
CITY

CREATING PEACE OF MIND IN
THE MIDST OF URBAN CHAOS

EDITED BY

ANGELA DEWS

Skyhorse Publishing

Skyhorse Publishing books may be purchased in bulk at special discounts for sales promotion, corporate gifts, fund-raising, or educational purposes. Special editions can also be created to specifications. For details, contact the Special Sales Department, Skyhorse Publishing, 307 West 36th Street, 11th Floor, New York, NY 10018 or info@skyhorsepublishing.com.

Skyhorse® and Skyhorse Publishing® are registered trademarks of Skyhorse Publishing, Inc.®, a Delaware corporation.

Visit our website at www.skyhorsepublishing.com.

10 9 8 7 6 5 4 3 2 1

Library of Congress Cataloging-in-Publication Data is available on file.

Cover design by Rain Saukas

Print ISBN: 978-1-5107-3233-9
Ebook ISBN: 978-1-5107-3234-6

Printed in the United States of America

Still, in the City is a collection of stories about the fierce practice of urban Buddhism—when a New York City subway becomes a mobile temple, when Los Angeles traffic becomes a vehicle for awakening, when a Fifth Avenue sidewalk becomes a gauntlet through craving, generosity, and sorrow.

Two dozen Buddhist teachers offer stories that are accessible, whether you've practiced a lot or a little—or are curious or maybe even cynical.

The authors represent a particular commitment to expanding access to the teachings for diverse communities. And our very presence on our cushions belies the notion that western Buddhists are of an age and race and class.

We have been asked not how to meditate, but why, by a neighbor who says the world is on fire and a friend whose work is seemingly holding up as much of that world as he can touch. We answer: there is amazing clarity in stillness, and the opportunity for a skillful response, rather than a reaction, even to injustice. And there is the possibility of equanimity and of freedom.

These are our stories in our own language in our own time.

With appreciation to Peg Moran for first draft editing and flow of *Still*.

CONTENTS

Contents

DHARMA, TRUTH

Contents

Contents

Dedicated to our teachers
Eugene Cash, Gina Sharpe, Thanissara, and Larry Yang,
and honoring especially Gina and Larry,
who continue to make the road by walking for diversity
and inclusion in the teaching of the dharma in the West.

FOREWORD

by Eugene Cash, Gina Sharpe, Larry Yang, and Thanissara

As teachers and guides of the two-year Community Dharma Leader Training of 2010 to 2012 at Spirit Rock Meditation Center, California, we are gratified and heartened by the publication of "Still, in the City." This nourishing and practical anthology, which arose from that training, carries the voices, hearts, and wisdom of a diverse, authentic and gifted group of authors who offer us important insights into living well and staying balanced in the midst of complexity, chaos, and confusion.

This book is not only a marvelous offering to all who navigate the sidewalks, subway, streets, and daily life business of New York City, or in fact, any city, from Atlanta to Johannesburg, Vancouver to Brazil; it also opens into a depth of soul, peace, and liminal transcendent potential that is the birthright of every human being, wherever we live.

The inspiration for this work arises from a very different world, that of the Indo-Gangetic Plains of India 2,600 years ago, where one of the world's great spiritual teachers, Shakyamuni Buddha, illuminated essential teachings and practices that cut to the core of the human condition.

The Buddha's crucial message, "Mind is the forerunner of all things," points to our task. It is to the mind we must go to remove or at least dampen the impulses of greed, hatred, and delusion, recognize the deeper realities of existence, and foster the potential we all have for wise seeing and compassionate action.

Although the physical and technological conditions of the Buddha's time and that of a modern city are vastly different, these vital, timeless teachings are pertinent for everyone regardless of time and place. To have this ancient road map applied to and reflected in our deeply challenging times is the tremendous gift of this outstanding book.

INTRODUCTION

by Angela Dews

In *Still, in the City*, we offer the stories that make ours an urban *dharma*—
in cities like New York and Los Angeles; Seattle and Pretoria; Anápolis,
Brazil; Oakland; and Victoria, BC. And in places that are called "terrible
cities," where the prison experience is particular, but reveals much about
deep practice and shared respect when living together.

*When terms are used in more than one chapter or need further explanation or
translation, they are included in the Notes and Links section at the back of the book.*

Our experience of practice in cities offers occasions for finding refuge,
of course, but also for awakening from the illusion of separation—the way
we were taught by our teachers who were taught by their teachers in
Southeast and South Asia in the 1960s and 70s. And we offer the intention to explicitly pay attention to suffering in relationships, including the
greed, hatred, and delusion that manifest as prejudice and injustice.

We have arranged the stories under three headings: the "Three Jewels,"
or Triple Gem, as it is often called. And we use the setting for the jewels
offered by teacher Tara Brach, that is, Buddha, awareness; *Dharma*, truth;
Sangha, love.

Buddha, Awareness

We are sharing our experience and the teachings of the human being
called Prince Siddhartha, who discovered, not invented, a way to find

freedom out of suffering for himself and for all beings over 2,500 years ago. And when he became the Buddha—the Enlightened One—he taught what he discovered with the admonition not to blindly accept anything but to see for ourselves.

The instructions offered here for exploring mindfulness in and around our cities are written to be accessible to a broad range of readers, whether you've practiced a lot or a little. Or, perhaps you practice mindfulness and don't call it Buddhism.

We start with meditation as the primary tool for investigating the nature of experience.

In the *Satipaṭṭhana Sutta*, which we offer in the *Dharma* section, the Buddha offers this invitation to find a place for contemplation of the breath in the body—the first of the Four Foundations of Mindfulness:

Here . . . , gone to the forest, or to the root of a tree, or to an empty hut, one sits down.

Already I can feel the push back. Forests and empty huts in the overwhelm and onslaught of the city? And, in fact, when the New York Insight Meditation Center was being created in the Flatiron District of Manhattan, one teacher suggested the meditation hall should be soundproof.

In addition to being impossible, creating a soundproof cocoon would defeat the purpose—the purpose of taking a seat in the center of a world that is demanding and full of distraction, and from that space letting the sounds land and linger and flow into the moments full of the absence of sound.

Besides, even in a soundproof room, the thoughts and the stories we make out of thoughts would still be swinging through the monkey mind.

That's how it was for Meghiya, one of the Buddha's attendants, who found the perfect pleasant and charming mango grove to meditate in, but when he finally sat down there he experienced sensual thoughts, malevolent thoughts, and cruel thoughts. The Buddha described the experience:

> . . . *trivial thoughts, subtle thoughts, mental jerkings that follow one along. Not understanding these mental thoughts, one runs back and forth with wandering mind.*

That's what minds do. The Buddha instructs us to note the arising of thought—Meghiya's trivial thought, for example—being aware that it is present, noting what led to its arising, and even noting the absence of thought.

When I sit on my own cushion in morning meditation, allowing space in my mind as the day begins, I can find amazing clarity. However, some days it feels as though there's no time and too much to do.

On the days when I succumb to those distractions, I often leave my job in Rockefeller Center, with my phone on a meditation app on vibrate, and I sit in a pew in St. Patrick's Cathedral surrounded by believers and splendor. It's a grand space in which to meditate and I am grateful and I leave a contribution.

When I walk out, I'm on Fifth Avenue, and I am barreling around the slow walkers and being busy being where I'm going and not where I am. And then I notice. And I have my practice to bring me home.

My first teacher, Vietnamese monk and teacher and peace activist Venerable Thich Nhat Hanh (Thay), taught me to walk and know that I am walking: *"I have arrived. I am home in the here and in the now,"* he said. There is contentment in landing in the present. But there is also the messiness.

One of the department stores that takes up a whole Fifth Avenue block is decked out to beguile and entice me. In one window, a fantasy presents a shoe that costs more than my rent, and it catches my attention, and I love it. I came to New York to see such things. I can find it beautiful without needing to own it, like a sunset or the lilac in a backyard where I don't live anymore. The Second Noble Truth states that suffering has a cause. I don't suffer when I can abandon my craving, when I am not wanting things to be different than they are. The Four Noble Truths teach the cause of suffering and the way out.

But.

When I open my awareness beyond my interior processes to the world that I am creating and sharing a space in, I see a sign. *"Help me,"* it asks. Those flagship stores also form a backdrop for people camped on the sidewalk on cardboard and plastic, alone or in couples, with pets and sometimes a child. And in that moment, I get to see once more that I am wanting things to be different than they are.

Throughout the Buddha's teachings, *Mara* appears. He is the embodiment of greed and hatred and delusion. And when he shows up, the Buddha says, "I see you, *Mara*." In that moment, I see *Mara* on Fifth Avenue. I see the way anger and sorrow and, yes, judgment, land and churn in my body. In that moment, I need to feel it. To tamp it down is to inhabit the even more dangerous place of denial and spiritual bypass. One of my *sangha* asked, where does the anger go if I let it go? Good question. I tell her, the causes and conditions for its arising are not outside of me, and when I no longer hold them, it goes back into the pool of anger, which is not mine.

After one session of yoga and meditation, a seventeen-year-old in a Brooklyn detention center told his teacher, "I never knew I wasn't my anger."

That comprehension—however fleeting—is the first step to the huge freedom of not making a familiar self out of the thoughts and feelings that land like silent sounds on the heart/mind (*citta*), which is the Buddha's sixth sense.

And I have tools.

Generosity meets my aversion and judgment. One of my teachers asked a man who was living on the sidewalk in her neighborhood what he needed when he asked her to help him. He said he would like pancakes for breakfast, please. She went to the diner and brought him some back. I have never done that, but now that I know it is possible, perhaps I will someday.

Lovingkindness and compassion meet my aversion and my anger. Yes. I am angry at the inequality and I am also averse. I am inclined to weigh the worth of the need and to devalue these strangers, based on their tribes and their circumstances. It's something I learned, and the social/economic order continues to teach and encourage. If I can recognize the causes and conditions for the perceptions and reactions, I can find compassion for them and for me. But to do that I must pause. No small thing. Because the anger is pushing me to a familiar place where I am powerless and deluded.

Discernment and wisdom meet my delusion. Thai Forest teacher Ajahn Chah pointed to a boulder and asked his monks, "Is it heavy?" They answered, "Yes, venerable sir." He said, "Only if you pick it up." The discernment is to know what I am obliged to take up. I remember my grandmother, the daughter of a man who was enslaved as a boy, asking me "What did you expect?" when I was yelling about some outrage that had happened in the nation. "Justice," I shouted. And she just walked out of the room, shaking her head. The wisdom is to know that there can be a different response than yelling or futility to the suffering of injustice, inequality, and violence. And what those responses might be for an engaged Buddhist.

Still, in the City offers stories that illustrate how the skills we learn from the Buddha and other wise ones allow us to see what we are experiencing, and to stand under the suffering. Then, to respond and to incline toward kindness when we act. The skills are wisdom and compassion and we need them both. Thankfully, they go together.

The next stage beyond the moment-to-moment awareness is inquiring, taking action, and changing habit patterns—this is where we meet such related practices as the *paramis*, or perfections of the heart.

It's no small thing. It took an ascetic called Sumedho, the being who would become Gautama Buddha, four incalculable periods and one hundred thousand eons to find freedom from greed, hatred, and delusion by developing these qualities during his past lifetimes that would take him to enlightenment. Those past lives are illustrated in Jataka tales, a body of literature recounting the prior lives of the Buddha when he was sometimes an animal—a goat, a frog, a deer. He was also often a merchant or other city dweller.

One tale is particularly apt. It is perhaps the one that started him on the path to find freedom. A being was in a hell realm carrying enormous bags of heavy rocks, with no opportunity for rest. He was surrounded by others also suffering, but isolated, alone in their suffering, not connected. The tale goes on, as suffering does, but at one instant he looked up and saw an old man with his bag of rocks and thought, "If I took his bag for a moment he could rest." That moment was the instant when he turned toward freedom. The tale teaches his discovery of compassion and connection, and the dignity of being in this human life.

We are continuing the tradition of teaching through storytelling.

Dharma, Truth

The *Satipatthana Sutta* is the foundational text for the *Vipassana* Buddhist lineage we share. The Buddha's instructions in the *sutta* would have the practitioner develop or establish mindfulness through contemplation in four areas (*satipatthanas*).

. . . *one abides contemplating body* (*kaya*), which includes mindfulness meditations on the breath, the four postures, activities throughout the day, parts of the body, the four elements, and death meditations;

. . . *one abides contemplating feeling* (*vedana*), which includes pleasant/unpleasant/neutral sensations;

. . . *one abides contemplating heart/mind or consciousness* (*citta*), which includes states of mind and emotion;

. . . *one abides contemplating* (*dhammas*), which include mental qualities and analyses of experience through the teachings on the hindrances, the aggregates, the sense-spheres, the awakening factors, the 4 Noble Truths.

And the *sutta* gives us the essential qualities for awareness.

. . . *one abides . . . diligent, clearly knowing, and mindful* . . .

Diligence and clear comprehension are essential to the task of being in cities. Mindfulness is taught today as a practice to alleviate stress and to manage pain—to know and to be with what is. The mindfulness practice we share has an intention to train for deeper understanding and change. The Buddha called such diligence the necessary strength for returning to the object of meditation, to mindfulness, with balance and continuity, through all of what are called the ten thousand joys and the ten thousand sorrows of the journey.

. . . *one abides . . . free from desires and discontent* (*covetousness and grief*) . . .

Clinging to desire is one translation for the term *tanha*. But *tanha* is also translated as thirst. And the aspiration for freedom from that attachment, from our dependency on desire and views, is at the core of the practice. Perhaps having an addiction offers a fortunate opportunity to have places where our thirst is obvious. There, we find that parts of ourselves can be reclaimed rather than dismissed; instead of being an obstacle to our journey, they are our journey and that is why they have showed up.

. . . one abides contemplating the nature of arising . . . of passing away . . . of both arising and passing away . . .

When time-traveling through the changes in our towns, can we accept the constant flux of conditions and mind states, knowing that which is impermanent is inherently unreliable and unsatisfying?

. . . one abides contemplating internally, . . . externally, or both internally and externally . . .

At its core, this teaching refers to our capacity to know what is going on with us (internally), in the world around us (externally), and impersonally, beyond self (both internally and externally).

And, Larry Yang, one of our core CDL teachers (see below), takes it further: "*The ramifications to the larger community of external contemplation are enormous. In this later teaching is the social experience of individuals and communities. In it also lies the awareness not only of our own experience, but also the awareness of our impact on others and other communities, as well as awareness of the experiences of others.*"

Sangha, Love

The Buddha gave our friend Meghiya five qualities that bring maturity of awareness to a monk. The first is admirable people as friends, companions, and colleagues. The authors of *Still, in the City* are a *sangha* in the broadest sense. We are a few of the graduates of the Fourth Community Dharma Leaders (CDL) training, created by James Baraz and sponsored by the Spirit Rock Meditation Center.

However, our CDL4 teaching team—Larry Yang, Thanissara, Gina Sharpe, and Eugene Cash—revamped the curriculum, the way the program was delivered and to whom. One result is that CDL4 consisted of 38 percent people of color, compared to an average of 6 percent POC within three previous iterations.

Our intention is to gain knowledge and to cultivate wisdom through study of Buddhist texts and through examination of experience itself. In addition, some of us have added the bowing and chanting of a devotional practice that we share with millions of Buddhists around the world and have taken the *bodhisattva* vow to benefit all beings.

Japanese poet Izumi Shikibu says: *"Watching the moon at midnight, solitary, mid-sky, I knew myself completely, no part left out."* The moon is a symbol of awakening in Zen Buddhism. The poet is contemplating the moon and she is contemplating the fullness of herself. No part left out. Her poem challenges me to know that I can't leave things outside the door in order to make my meditation space safe and in order to blend in. So, I can love the silence and also love practicing in community, which allows me to develop the capacity to be with suffering and to develop compassion, equanimity, and, yes, love.

There are two truths. There is a universal truth that we are all connected, there are no separate selves, and putting a name on things fractures the universe. There's also the relative truth of how we live together. People live with the truth of gender, sexual orientation, race and culture, age, and with a disability, and those are the conditions of our experience and our communities. They are concepts and views, so, they get to be defined by the user, consciously or unconsciously.

The authors represent a particular commitment to reconnecting and listening to learn what those conditions and experiences mean. We are developing community-based *sanghas* and expanding access to the teachings for diverse communities.

The summer day we chose for a "Day of Mindfulness" in New York City happened to be the same day the Big Apple Barbecue Block Party fed over one hundred thousand in Madison Square Park, and a Hari Krishna parade danced its way down Fifth Avenue with chants and drums and cymbals thumping and ringing as soundtrack.

On the other side of the Avenue, thirty of us walked slowly together through the smoke and smells and sounds with the monks and nuns from Blue Cliff Monastery, Thich Nhat Hanh's upstate New York refuge and practice center. Afterwards, one of Thay's monks asked us how we "householders" hold our mindfulness practice in a crowded city.

We answered: *"The crowd is made up of single people and we send love to each one of them;* Sangha *is essential; and today, it is easy to see that the fruits of our practice benefitted all beings."*

Those answers and the answers we share in *Still, in the City* speak to the deep settling that is possible.

BUDDHA, AWARENESS

TREES IN THE CITY

by Margo McLoughlin

Like all great teachers and poets, the Buddha knew the value of a good metaphor. He presented concepts like desire and restlessness, faith and generosity, by drawing comparisons to familiar sights and experiences in nature. In the *Dhammapada*, the fickle mind is compared to a fish on dry land, flapping this way and that, or to a bird alighting wherever it wants. Craving is a creeping vine, the result of which are sorrows, growing like wild grass. In the *Saddha Sutta*, a banyan tree serves as a metaphor for one who is consummate in faith:

> Just as a large banyan tree, on level ground where four roads meet, is a
> haven for the birds all around, even so a lay person of conviction is a
> haven for many people: monks, nuns, male lay followers, and female lay
> followers.

The Buddha's creative use of metaphor encourages us to sharpen our own perception and see the metaphorical potential in our everyday lives.

Look out from where you find yourself right now. Are any trees visible in your sight line? Let yourself take in their color and shape. Are you able to distinguish any particular features, like the texture of the bark, or the pattern of the leaves or needles? If they are close enough, perhaps there are sounds or even smells that give the tree more than just a visual presence in the landscape or cityscape. The sight (and smell and sound) of trees in an urban landscape has the potential not just to refresh the mind in the way that nature refreshes; it can also serve to link us with the Buddha's teachings on practice.

In the discourse on the Four Foundations of Mindfulness, the *Satipatthana Sutta*, the Buddha gives very clear instructions on how to establish mindfulness: the practitioner or *bhikkhu* goes to a forest grove, to the root of a tree, or to an empty hut, and sits down cross-legged, with spine erect. Breathing in, they know they are breathing in. Breathing out, they know they are breathing out. Mindfulness is a training of the mind that begins with this knowing what is happening in the present moment, not just in the general sense of knowing what we are doing as we go about our day, but in a very specific way—knowing an inhalation, versus an exhalation, knowing a short breath versus a long breath. In order to develop continuity of mindfulness, a degree of seclusion from the distractions of life plays an important role. The forest grove offers that seclusion.

As inheritors of the Buddha's teachings, students in the Western world have created wonderful retreat centers outside of the urban environment where the stillness and quiet of a forest grove offer nourishing conditions for establishing inner quiet and clear-seeing. In subtle ways, this sets up a dichotomy. We begin to view retreat in a secluded leafy environment as the only suitable condition for deepening our practice. But what if we applied the Buddha's own skillful use of metaphor to our urban lives? What if we expanded our definition of the conditions laid out in the *Satipatthana Sutta*? Is it possible to develop continuity of mindfulness and deepen our practice right here in the city?

Let us begin with the forest grove. Truly, the forest is a balm to the spirit, offering a stark contrast to the cacophony of the urban world. In the forest, on a windy day, currents of air comb the branches of the conifers, rippling the leaves of the deciduous trees, weaving a symphony of sound, complete with crescendos, decrescendos, and the sudden appearance of birdsong or the distinct background melody of water moving over rocks. Subtle scents (think pine needles on a forest path, warmed by sunlight) embrace us and we naturally breathe more deeply in this richly oxygenated landscape.

But in the absence of a wild forest, or even a park with trees, our practice invites us to find the forest right here in the city. What if we could train the heart/mind to recognize our own potential in the moment of perceiving a tree? *Ah, there is my forest grove. Let me begin again right now and re-establish mindfulness in my life.* The formulation of this thought takes a certain amount of time and feels cumbersome at first, but with practice it may be possible to evoke the association in the very moment of seeing. Perception is followed by remembering. As the eyes take in the experience of a tree, a strong association is developed, one that will be unique to each of us as practitioners of the Buddha's teachings. For some, there may be a recollection of previous experiences of practice in forested retreat environments, or there may be a strong image of the Buddha taking his seat under the Bodhi tree on the night of his awakening.

To wake up in the midst of city life requires knowing the conditions you are working with. Cities, by definition, are a glorious smorgasbord of competing distractions. Everywhere we turn, sights, sounds, and smells call to our senses. A lot of it is advertising, pure and simple. If we pay attention, we may notice how some images and sounds trigger an immediate feeling of desire, pulling us in one direction or another. That is the whole game of advertising—to set off a desire and nudge you towards fulfilling it. Images of a can of beer glistening with condensation, or even the image of a pristine mountain lake, are designed to make you want something you don't have, propelling you into a possible future where that desire is satisfied (and a new one is born).

In a city, we can easily lose track of where we're going and how we're living this precious human birth. Yet there are ways of remembering. We can train our minds to recognize the trees in our urban environment as "advertising" for mindfulness, planted and cared for by city crews, not just to refresh the spirit, offering shade and beauty, but also to gently remind us of something we already have—the potential to be present in our lives, the potential to wake up.

The trees you happen upon as you go about your day, let them whisper to you the story of the Buddha on the night he took his seat under the Bodhi tree, making his resolve to awaken for the benefit of beings. The upright trunk of a tree evokes the image of the Buddha setting his spine erect. In Pali, the word is *uju*, with connotations of steadfastness. A tree's very immovability inspires us to emulate the Buddha in his unshakability of mind, even as *Mara*, the personification of desire, challenged him with every sensual desire. The city is the realm of Mara, but within that realm we can keep our eyes open for another kind of appearance—the swaying or fluttering of green trees in city parks, large and small, and the lines of trees planted along the boulevard.

We can store up associations, deepen and expand the power of this living metaphor, so that any and every encounter with a tree waters the seed of our intention to practice wisdom and compassion. How? Through spending time in the company of these great beings we call trees, receiving their teachings, and calling to mind the Buddha's instructions—go to a forest grove, to the root of a tree, establish mindfulness before you, through getting to know particular trees in your neighborhood, and even taking an active role in caring for them.

The City of New York now has a website dedicated to the trees of the urban forest, the Tree Map of New York. The purpose of the site is clearly to invite stewardship of the trees that line the streets of the city. Visitors can register, returning to the site to keep track of where their favorite trees are located. Tips for tree care, from watering and weeding, to adding mulch and learning how to prune, remind us that caring for the trees around us is a learnable skill. (Visit https://tree-map.nycgovparks.org.)

Another way to extend and explore this metaphor is to see trees as manifestations of the triple gem—the Buddha, the *dhamma*, and the *sangha*. In some Buddhist traditions, at the beginning of a day of practice, we chant the refuges and precepts, often in Pali:

> *Buddham saranam gacchami.*
> *Dhammam saranam gacchami.*
> *Sangham saranam gacchami.*
> *I go to the Buddha for refuge.*
> *I go to the Dhamma for refuge.*
> *I go to the Sangha for refuge.*

What does it mean to take refuge? A refuge is a place of shelter and protection, especially in a storm. By taking refuge in the Buddha, the *dhamma*, and the *sangha*, we acknowledge our vulnerability to the winds of fortune, to the truth of aging, illness, and death. We remember there is a safe harbor and this path of practice that sustains and nourishes us.

Tree as Buddha—
I take refuge in trees as a reminder of my own potential

To take refuge in the Buddha is to take refuge in the historical figure, a prince of the Sakyan clan, who set out to understand what drives the round of birth and death. But it also invites a more personal meaning. The word "Buddha" means "one who is awake." When we take refuge in the Buddha we are remembering our own potential to liberate the mind.

Tree as Buddha suggests many possible connections. We can each build our own associations, layering our experience of trees into a sustaining metaphor.

Some years ago, I attended a conference on the role of storytelling in the work of truth-telling and reconciliation. The conference was held at the University of British Columbia in Vancouver, in a building on the edge of campus surrounded by mature cedar trees. The panel included speakers who had worked with Archbishop Desmond Tutu on the Truth and Reconciliation Commission in South Africa. As well, there were indigenous leaders from British Columbia who spoke about the traumatic legacy of the Indian residential school system, in which aboriginal children were forcibly removed from their families to attend boarding schools run by Christian churches. In the audience, there were a number of residential school survivors who voiced their despair at the ongoing impact of that experience on themselves, their families, and their communities. A professor from the University of Victoria's school of Indigenous Governance acknowledged their pain and welcomed their stories, listening carefully and then encouraging them to seek solace and comfort in the cedar trees that stood nearby. If the hearings triggered strong emotions, she said, they could step outside and stand in the presence of the trees, touching the bark, stroking the cedar fronds, taking in the scent of cedar boughs, and moving beyond a story of personal suffering to a reminder of shared heritage and meaning rooted in the natural world.

Tree as *Dhamma*—I take refuge in the wisdom of trees

Taking refuge in trees as manifestations of the Buddha is taking refuge in their sheltering generosity, while taking refuge in trees as *dhamma* is remembering the wisdom teachings that trees impart to us all year long, perhaps especially teachings on *anicca*, impermanence. Is there a tree in your life that you observe through the changing seasons? Where I live in Victoria, the shaggy chestnut trees that line many city streets are forever drawing my attention: in spring their leaves open up like green parasols; next come their towering candelabra blossoms; and in autumn, they drop such surprising treasures, spiky green husks splitting open to reveal the glossy nuts inside. One of these great chestnuts, whose massive trunk showed the movement of its yearly growth, twisting and turning towards the light, was there one day, providing shade at a local café, and the next only a stump remained. It had been cut down by city crews and carried away, because of rot and the danger of falling limbs. Like us, trees have a lifespan. They remind us that change is also a narrative of death and transformation.

In a small art gallery on Vancouver Island, more than seventy people have crowded in to watch a dance performance. In their choreographed movements, the six dancers tell the story of the great trees that fall in the forest, returning over the decades to the earth, providing nourishment to countless other beings. Renée Poisson, the sculptor and videographer whose work is at the center of the exhibit, had decided to inquire into the act of falling as a way to explore her own aging and to prepare for that transformation. At intervals, over the course of several years, she set up a camera and filmed herself falling onto the soft, heathery slopes of a nearby mountain. She went into the forest and observed the fallen maple, cedar, hemlock, and fir, out of whose rotting trunks other trees were already growing. She chose several long limbs of local wood and wood from other continents and carved immense staffs, sanding and polishing the surface to a soft smoothness, inviting visitors to stroke and lift the wood. I watched a group of children crowd around as Renée explained her process, and then begin lifting and gently rearranging the staffs on the floor of the main gallery, while others went into a nearby room to film themselves falling on mats.

Tree as *Sangha*—
honoring the reciprocal relationship we have with trees

Last, when we take refuge in trees as part of our community, our *sangha,* we enlarge our understanding of what *sangha* means to us. Traditionally, *sangha* referred to the community of ordained monks and nuns. Now, it more often refers to our local community of *dharma* practitioners or to all those who are engaged in the work of awakening. To see the trees as part of our *sangha* means letting go of distinctions that separate living beings into categories. It is a way of honoring the reciprocal relationship we have with trees. *Breathing in, I am grateful to the trees that clean the air and provide life-giving oxygen. Breathing out, I undertake to honor the trees in my life and the trees on this planet.*

By taking refuge in trees as *sangha,* we bow to their unique beauty, wisdom teachings, and selfless generosity. We allow ourselves to be supported and nourished by their presence in our lives. When we are feeling disconnected, lost, or confused, it may be that all we need is to look out a window or go out to a local park and let our gaze fall on a quiet green sentinel, a beech, a birch, an elm, a fir, a cedar, a pine, a hemlock, a willow, a cherry, a chestnut, a maple, or any old anonymous tree, sending its roots into the earth and reminding us, as it reaches and grows towards the sky, that our training in awareness can happen anywhere. The forest grove of the Buddha is alive in the trees of the city.

THE HAWKS IN OUR HEARTS: YOU *ARE* NATURE

by Sebene Selassie

One morning I was walking Suki in the small park near our apartment. She was off-leash looking for squirrels and I was entangled in thoughts about my day. At first, I did not realize that I was caught up in my usual planning and plotting. Speeding around the loop on autopilot, I was only semi-aware of Suki and otherwise lost in a current of increasing mental tension. At some point, I noticed the momentum and constriction of my mind and heart and stopped in my tracks.

My first thought was "Get it together, woman! You're a mindfulness teacher!" My second was "What do you sense right now?"

Sati, the Pali word we've translated as "mindfulness" (unfortunately leading us to believe it's all about the head), also means awareness and memory, and has a strong foundation in the body and senses. When I finally noticed my speeding mind and body, I paused. I was *remembering* to be *aware*. Not that I cannot plan, but in the previous moment I was *lost and caught up in thoughts*. I was not actually aware that I was planning (and because of that, probably not that successful at it).

When mindfulness kicked in, I instructed myself to be present to that moment by noticing sensations both internal and external. I felt my breath in the belly and my feet on the ground and then I looked around me. As if for the first time, I saw the small fountain that soaks neighborhood kids in the summer. It is actually a beautiful metal sculpture and the artist echoed the shape and texture of a tree—perhaps that tree right in front of it. I scanned the tree from the bottom up. I finally saw it. A hawk at the very top. Looking straight at me.

A hawk. In Crown Heights, Brooklyn. Awe. Wonder. Mystery. Beauty.

Nature is all around us. Even in stinky, dirty New York City. In the sky above, and the cracks below. And what came to me as I looked at that hawk—knowing it could see me, in more ways than one, far better than I it—is that *nature is also in us*. In my busyness, I miss the hawks in the trees. And I miss the hawks in my heart. The simple acts of seeing and knowing that allow me to connect with this creature above me; the simplicity and profundity of acknowledging a moment. The awe, wonder, mystery, beauty within.

I AM nature. We ARE nature.

As a black woman in America, that's a radical statement. We don't get identified with nature in ways that inspire this sense of awe and beauty. Even though black people have been connected to this particular land for centuries, that *dignity* (as Frantz Fanon describes the relationship) has been denied us. It is reserved for white people to be in deep relationship with American nature; to enjoy, destroy, and now save (or it is fetishized as a uniquely innate talent of Native Americans to be one with nature).

I stood there in the park that day with my domesticated dog whose instincts draw her to scramble after smaller creatures; and, who, when I yell commands, halts that drive and returns to me, content. Staring up at this wild something in the city with Suki at my side, I was reminded of the wild in me, and that which is gentle and still. All three of us and the creatures above and below and around us, all belonging to this moment.

Last fall, I visited San Francisco Insight and Eugene Cash read the poem *Wilderness* by Carl Sandburg. The poem reveals the animals within (wolf, fox, hog, fish, eagle)—wild and natural, regal and base. This is the last stanza:

> *O, I got a zoo, I got a menagerie, inside my ribs, under my bony head, under my red-valve heart—and I got something else: it is a man-child heart, a woman-child heart: it is a father and mother and lover: it came from God-Knows-Where: it is going to God-Knows-Where—For I am the keeper of the zoo: I say yes and no: I sing and kill and work: I am a pal of the world: I came from the wilderness.*

We all came from the wilderness. We all belong to it. And to each other.

SONDER, IN THE CITY

by Gary Singer

As a native New Yorker, I tend to think of this city as a giant petri dish, in which some of the greatest breakthroughs, inventions, and audacious ideas have been nurtured to fruition. Just like the boundary line between sea and shore contains the greatest nutrients, the sheer number of disparate people from the far-flung corners of the earth congregating so close together that we can smell each other, we New Yorkers are constantly mixing in a glorious ongoing dance of miscegenation. We're continually bumping up against each other, rubbing off on each other, and leaving telltale marks.

It's against this backdrop of continual renewal and exchange that I've developed a *dhamma* practice that I had a tough time naming until just this morning when I saw something like it on the website called *The Dictionary of Obscure Sorrows:*

sonder

n. the realization that each random passerby is living a life as vivid and complex as your own—populated with their own ambitions, friends, routines, worries, and inherited craziness—an epic story that continues invisibly around you, in which you might appear only once, as an extra sipping coffee in the background, as a blur of traffic passing on the highway, as a lighted window at dusk.

So first, a bit of background.

Central to the Buddha's teachings are the *three characteristics*: *Anicca*, *Dukkha*, and *Anatta*.

Anicca, or change, is always, everywhere. Nothing is static, not even the subway car as it's stuck between stations. To the degree to which we don't see this and therefore try to hold onto what by nature cannot be held onto, we suffer.

Dukkha, translated as suffering or dissatisfaction or stress, is also everywhere we turn. Even when we get exactly what we want, in time our delight turns to dissatisfaction. And in the drive to want new or more or better, ultimately, we come to realize that "getting more" only brings us more dissatisfaction. *Dukkha* is waiting around the corner.

The third characteristic, *Anatta*, in some ways, is the hardest idea to embrace. Translated as "not self," it points to the reality that even while we might have a solid sense of who we are, there is no solid self that we can point to and hold on to. Even our selves are undergoing constant, if subtle, changes all the time. And the more we insist on holding onto a solid "me, I, and mine," the more *dukkha* we experience.

This slavish loyalty to bolstering our sense of identity is one of the cornerstones of dissatisfaction. How much energy it takes for us to continually project and protect our identities out in the world! As the Zen master Roshi Suzuki says, "All Judgment is odious because it wipes out the uniqueness of another person." The comparing/judging mind is like a lighthouse, casting assessments and judgments, nonstop, 360 degrees. As soon as the eye makes contact, the cascade of conception begins. First, we make contact with another, and in nanoseconds, the mind assesses, evaluates, judges, and then renders the judgment: better or lesser than me.

The Buddha talks of our tendency to engage in *manna* or measuring/comparing. Left to its own devices, the mind measures ourselves against others as better, worse, or equal to them. While we might think judging that we're better at least gives us the benefit of feeling superiority, we're still building up the brittle sense of "me." We can try to define ourselves in any number of ways, but according to the teachings, we still wind up separating this sense of self from others. And in the rush to identify differences, we lose the awareness that we have far more in common than we have differences. And this clinging to measuring and differences leads us to yet another form of dissatisfaction.

This continual beacon of judgment takes its toll. Just the act of comparing is *dukkha*. In that moment of measuring, we're cut off from the other, whether feeling inferior or superior, we wind up separate and alone. But because this happens so constantly and quickly, we're not even aware of the self-imposed prison of the ego. This feeling of isolation can breed a sense of unworthiness as it fixes our sense of self and other.

Perhaps this is what the teacher Charlotte Joko Beck alludes to when she says "'To enjoy the world without judgment is what a realized life is like."

Yet, we can't stop comparing: that's just what the mind does. Spurred on by evolution's edict to survive, the mind had to develop a way to quickly determine if something was dangerous or not, categorizing all things as either "good" or "bad" to survival. Today, the mind continues to react in this self-protective way—we call it judgment—but we can be mindful of the chronic comparing and counteract it.

When I first learned about the habitual patterns of the comparing mind, I was shocked to learn how often and quickly the mind reverts to manna. With a microsecond glance, the mind has compared, rendered a judgment, and moved on. In fact, I couldn't sense a time when I wasn't judging, leaving me exhausted, brittle, and very alone.

This is where sondering becomes a tool of awareness and a way out of this manna trap. As I move through the city, I reflect on how everyone around me is playing a supporting role to my starring role in my own life. And, at the same time, I'm a bit player to everyone around me. The mutuality of our roles in each other's lives shines a light on the reality that each of us has a rich depth, unknowable to one another.

But what is known is that each of us places ourselves at the center of our lives. As I move through the city, I imagine each of us is a solar system of our own making. We place ourselves as the sun around which orbit all the people and things that make up our lives. Those closest to ourselves are in the nearest orbits; those farther away, in more distant orbits. I imagine each person as having rings around them, populated by relationships of all kinds. And in this way, each of us occupies our own universe. As we walk past each other, our universes continually brush up against each other. And if we talk to someone, those universes begin to interact.

Reflecting on this, several things become clearer. First is the recognition that while everyone around me appears to be an extra, they are in fact the stars of their own lives, just like me. This begins the softening of the comparing and judging mind, as it realizes that we each share the star/extra roles simultaneously.

As I intentionally imagine orbits around each person, I get a sense of the richness, depth, and breadth of their lives. No longer do they appear as extras, but as stars in their own right, each with their own epic life stories, each—like me—living at the center of their own universes. While the details of their stories may differ from my own, their lives are really no different from mine. We each are grappling with our ambitions, successes, failures, joys, and sorrows.

This growing sense of commonality leads to a greater sense of humility as it softens the barrier between "me" and "others." At the same time, a growing sense of empathy dawns on me, as I realize there really is very little that separates me from others. That most of what I think of as differences is really how much I choose to emphasize those differences. I could just as easily dwell on our commonalities, but isn't it interesting how I tend to emphasize the contrasts. Through sondering, the illusion of separation begins to dispel.

That developing empathy and the recognition of our commonalities then yield to a growing compassion. I remember one day walking up the stairs from the subway platform to the street. As I went up, I noticed an elderly woman making her way down, hobbling with trepidation. My first response—unlooked for—was "Grandma! Let me help her." Of course, she wasn't my grandmother, but in that instant, it didn't matter. She was *someone's* grandmother and therefore, she was mine. I approached her and walked her down to the subway platform. The appearance of self and other had softened; in response, the heart naturally followed.

This wasn't an instance of reminding myself to be generous or helpful. In the moment, my action seemed instinctual; after all, she was someone's grandma, all grandmas, my grandma. It was a sudden recognition, when I was able to open my perspective to include all people around me and their universes, that led me to automatically want to help her.

And this is the power of the Buddha's teachings turned to practice. The opening of the heart, so essential to the practice, came so naturally, once having sondered. In psychological language, it's called "de-centering": taking yourself out of the central role in your life to expand your perspective, to understand others better, and to quiet the ongoing demands of the ego. And, with most mindful-related efforts, just remembering to do it is where most of the effort is. And what a payoff.

DARE WE LEAVE OUR BUDDHIST CENTERS?

by Harrison Blum

How can mindfulness be an ally to the oppressed, and not just a relaxation fad for the privileged?

Mindfulness is hot. It's now taught from prisons to boardrooms, with championship NBA teams and with kindergarteners. In early 2014, Amazon.com listed around two thousand books for sale with the word *mindfulness* in the title. Three years later there were over seven thousand.

Amidst the mindfulness boom, not enough people are asking who's benefiting, and who's being left out.

Because I live just a few miles from the heart of Boston, biking has been my daily form of urban transportation for close to fifteen years. Cruising through the city streets provides a unique lens into how close seemingly separate neighborhoods and organizations actually are. In a five-minute bike ride, I could pass the most affluent houses in Cambridge as well as its housing projects, a meditation center serving the highly educated and a community center serving people living in poverty.

This proximity of such disparate life experiences helped clarify for me that, beyond enticing greater racial and class diversity *into* our meditation centers, we must *leave* the walls of these centers to be better neighbors across our cities and towns. The focus must shift from *inviting in* to *going out*. The Mindfulness Allies Project (MAP) provides a model to do that.

In the fall of 2014, I attended the International Symposium for Contemplative Studies, one of the world's biggest conferences examining mindfulness with the likes of the Dalai Lama offering keynotes. Just 5 percent of the more than three hundred featured talks and posters focused on race and class dynamics in the application of mindfulness and other contemplative practices.

While large-scale statistics are hard to come by, a high percentage of Western Buddhists and professional mindfulness providers are seemingly white, well-educated, and of middle or upper class. One study [Jacob et al. 2009] of over eight hundred people "with considerable experience with mindfulness meditation" found that 76 percent had received a graduate degree or completed some graduate school. The group's reported median household income was $70,000-80,000 per year, while the national median for that year was $46,326.

This isn't to say that people of color (POC) and people of low socioeconomic status (SES) aren't meditating. On the contrary, practice among these groups is growing. Looking specifically at the Insight Meditation tradition, one of the main forms of Buddhism in the West, the past ten years have seen an increase in regional Insight centers—especially urban ones—offering regular POC sitting groups. Insight Meditation's two main retreat centers, Insight Meditation Society (IMS) and Spirit Rock, offer annual POC retreats. Teacher training within the Insight community has also shifted toward greater diversity of teachers and served communities. Spirit Rock's fourth Community Dharma Leader (CDL) training (graduates of which have authored all chapters of this book) began in 2010 with an accepted class consisting of 38 percent people of color, compared to an average of 6 percent POC across three previous iterations of CDL and three iterations of a two-year Dedicated

Practitioner Program. The current Spirit Rock Teacher Trainees are majority POC, and the current IMS Teacher Training Program is comprised 75 percent of POC.

The IMS website's page on Commitment to Diversity states, *"We are clear that, if people of color feel IMS is just like many other predominantly white institutions in the country, then it cannot be a true spiritual refuge."* Insight can talk the talk, and increasingly, signs show that they can walk the walk.

Socioeconomic status is a somewhat different story. While some Insight centers offer need-based scholarships for programs or retreats, SES has yet to be addressed with the attention currently paid to race. This is a shame because, quite literally, poverty kills. The American Psychological Association holds that the stress of living with low SES can increase chances of cardiovascular disease and death. The impact of being a person of color experiencing pervasive overt and subtle racism can also lead to such psychological and medical risk.

So, what are we going to do about it? How can mindfulness be an ally to the oppressed, and not just a relaxation fad for the privileged? And in my case, what can a privileged white guy do to help?

Over two summers I piloted a potential response—the Mindful Allies Project. A queer, feminist ex-girlfriend helped me conceive idea, and anti-racism training I'd done helped me flesh it out.

In brief, MAP frames best practices for Western Buddhist teachers, as well as professional mindfulness providers, to secular mindfulness series in partnership with local organi marginalized populations, particularly in relation to race best practices include connecting with partner or teaching classes, sharing leadership roles with me

organizations, and training beyond mindfulness in practices and competencies such as anti-racism training, class awareness, feminism, nonviolent communication, and Insight Dialogue.

MAP is founded on a vision of mindfulness equity—or equal access to mindfulness teachings. Distinct from organizations already teaching mindfulness with low-income communities, such as the Holistic Life Foundation and the Lineage Project, MAP is based on an annual four- to six-week mindfulness series—a level of commitment small enough for mindfulness teachers to volunteer and large enough for participants to benefit. Sounds nice, right? It also works well!

For the MAP pilots, I led four to five weekly mindfulness classes at a community center serving low-income residents of Cambridge, with childcare, dinner, and Spanish-English translators also provided free of charge. Participants mostly consisted of people of color earning less than $15,000 per year. MAP quantitative and qualitative feedback was highly positive, and one participant even invited me to lead a mindfulness workshop with the lay ministers of her nearby evangelical Christian church. This initial success suggests the MAP model could benefit both marginalized communities and the Buddhist centers and teachers desiring to diversify those benefitting from their teachings in the West.

But you don't have to take my word for it. Here's some feedback from the participants themselves:

1. "I believe I learned to be more aware of different situations and have more acceptance and to be less judgmental. I learned that pain is inevitable. I knew it but I accepted it more as a part of life, not as a punishment."

    "Since the first class I learned how to deal with certain stressful situations. Now when I see myself getting stress I stop, pause, and clear my head."

3. "I don't get mad or irritated that easily with people I used to get mad at. I feel like a weight has been lifted off my shoulders; relationships are so much better."

4. "I feel at ease with myself, don't feel stressed as much, and I feel better with the new person I am becoming."

5. "I started to control and understand my chronic pain."

6. "It feels like I have this great secret that I share between my mind, heart & soul, and it makes me smile and feel love for myself, something that is very, very hard for me."

7. "Although I have taken similar classes before it wasn't until now . . . that I grasped the mindfulness meaning. For me it's the first step to beginning to love myself, something I have been trying for over fifty yrs."

This is all well and good, but beyond the positive impact of these initial pilots, for the MAP model to succeed it must be sustainable for meditation teachers. Each MAP class-week took about seven hours of work, divided among food shopping, cooking, class planning, class teaching, check-in emails and phone calls to participants, and printing handouts. I also spent about ten hours prior to each series connecting with leaders of the community center, promoting the series, and preparing a questionnaire. The total amount of time needed to create and run a MAP series is thus about forty-five hours.

Financially, it cost about $350 to produce. Half of these funds was used to provide childcare during and dinner after each class free of charge. The other half was used to provide ten-dollar Target gift cards for completing the questionnaire and to send each participant a copy of *The Power of Now* as a concluding gesture. Funding for this pilot series was drawn from *dana* (donations) from four previous Buddhist workshops I had offered.

Forty-five hours and $350 seem like reasonable contributions to be of service to local marginalized community members. If team-taught, responsibilities for a Buddhist center or mindfulness provider could be delegated and the hours divided. Whether Buddhist centers choose to embark upon such a project remains to be seen. Letters of introduction and invitations to participate in MAP, along with a hard copy of the MAP founding paper and a summary of the first pilot series, were mailed to IMS and Spirit Rock as well as to six of the largest urban Insight centers in the US. Only two responded, and none expressed interest in learning more or collaborating. At least one of these urban centers has an annual budget of over $100,000.

One possible reason for this poor response is reluctance by Buddhist centers to engage in teachings that are not strictly Buddhist. Yet, the growing interest in mindfulness, with its roots in Buddhist practice, presents an opportune moment for Buddhist organizations in the West to be among the forefront of innovative mindfulness interventions.

A second cause of the low interest could be that centers already have community service projects in place. For the most part, though, these focus on providing material assistance to those in need. While you can't feed a hungry person with meditation, Buddhist centers and mindfulness teachers are in a unique position to also offer something beyond material aid—the practices and fruits of mindfulness training.

A third, and more compelling, reason for these centers not to gravitate toward MAP could simply be that they're "not there yet." Buddhist centers, especially predominantly white ones, need to do their own self-reflective work to get woke and be safe spaces, especially before partnering with largely POC and low SES neighbors. POC groups can no longer be the only race-based affinity groups in our Buddhist centers. It's high time that white ally or white consciousness raising groups are also the norm.

Thankfully, the past five years have seen a spike in Buddhist centers, particularly urban ones, carving out time and space for their white meditators to do this work.

More Buddhists waking up to their own whiteness is a great thing, and as a community we're just beginning to take these steps. Maybe it's thus developmentally premature in the evolution of race awareness within Insight Meditation to broadly push the MAP model. Maybe it's better, for now, to focus more on whites getting woke, to lay that foundation for MAP, or something like it, in the future.

In the first MAP class a participant asked me, "Are you going to be teaching us meditation in a spiritual way?" I told her that I'd prefer not to respond, but would rather welcome her to answer that question upon completion of the series. When we arrived at the last class, I circled back to her question. "Well, you didn't teach meditation like it was a religious thing," she reflected, "but I found it deeply spiritual. I connected to my soul in a whole new way."

The Buddha classically advised not to teach without an invitation. What further invitation are we waiting for when science has documented the illness and higher mortality rates suffered at the hands of racism and poverty?

SIMPLY LIVING

by Alex Haley and Carissa Jean Tobin

I know I shouldn't be running because of my hip injury, but the thought "I really need to make my 8 a.m. meeting" pushes me to sprint. The bus pulls away from the stop just as I arrive. As I pull out my phone to look for the next bus, a police car roars by, its siren startling me into a vigilant attention. My phone shows me email notifications from work—three people are wondering why I haven't replied to their previous emails, and four more have sent me calendar invites for events, one happening two hours from now, and one six months down the road.

Life anywhere, worldwide, can be hectic. We live in an era of multitasking, twenty-four/seven hyper-connectedness and the pressure to do more.

Here in the city of Minneapolis, it's no different. In fact, seeing people walking down the street, riding on the bus—even driving their cars—as they frantically check their phones, eat breakfast, or groom themselves for the day is a constant reminder of the pace of life many of us are living.

And yet.

The Buddha's teachings emphasize that if we can live unburdened within the constantly changing dance of sights, sounds, smells, tastes, sensations, and mental experience, then joy arises; the Buddha referred to this as the joy of renunciation. This type of renunciation is not based upon deprivation or austerity; rather it's an inward journey of releasing our habits of projecting happiness externally or delaying happiness until some future date or state. Can we notice how often we're living from the unspoken belief that "if I get there / get this / get rid of this / get through this period of life, then I'll be at ease / happy / relaxed"? James Taylor said something similar when he sang, *"The secret of life is enjoying the passage of time."* This kind of renouncing is a stepping into the fullness and flow of life with a courageous and confident heart.

So how do we do that here in the city where everything is a rush of activity?

It's a constant negotiation, and one that my wife Carissa and I have undertaken. Not perfected by any means, but it's how we practice.

The following are some of our reflections on living simply in the city.

Uncluttered home, uncluttered mind

Carissa explains: (her statements and personal experiences are in italics): *We don't keep a lot of stuff around. We get rid of things that we don't use. This means that, visually, there is less clutter to make us feel agitated. There's not actually more space in our rooms, but there's more unfilled space. In fact, a friend came over for the first time and wondered if we actually lived here, because the environment looked so empty. We laughed and assured him that this was our home—sparseness and all.*

Keeping material possessions to a minimum in a consumption-based economy isn't easy. Of course, we are tempted to get the newest gadget to replace our seven-year-old laptop with the frayed cord. In order to keep things from accumulating, we have to be disciplined. Getting a new phone to replace the old one with the dying battery? Time for us to wipe the old one and recycle it. Not next week. Now.

Buddhists refer to this kind of unadorned living as an aspect of Right Livelihood (*sammaajiva*), which for laypeople is often discussed in terms of one's job or occupation, but is much more expansive. It includes *how* we live day-to-day (including all of the daily life choices we make) as much as *what* we do for a living. Speaking to the monastic community, the Buddha emphasized wise reflection upon the four requisites of the spiritual life: robes, almsfood, shelter for rest, and medicine. These requisites were to be used for the specific purpose of maintaining good health, offering protection, and supporting what was needed (versus wanted) for spiritual development. As laypeople, we have much more stuff beyond the four requisites; however, the Buddha's teaching of wise reflection upon what is really necessary is still just as relevant to us—what do we really need and what choices are we making that might be feeding the never-sated impulse to acquire, gain, and own more stuff? How does a lifetime of wanting, acquiring, and gaining affect the health of the planet and every living being on it? With less stuff, there is more physical space and (not coincidentally) more mental space.

Wise communities

The Buddhist Eightfold Path is not easy to follow on your own. The Buddha encouraged finding admirable friends and associating with the wise. He even provided laypeople with specific suggestions on how to do this— he said to seek out and follow the example of those people who were confident that spiritual awakening was possible (and who had confidence that the Buddha had done it), who upheld five ethical precepts in their life, who were generous, and who had developed wisdom. [AN 8:54] As is oft quoted, the Buddha replied to his attendant Ananda that having admirable friends is actually the whole of the holy life because having such friends leads a person to pursue the Eightfold Path. [SN 45:2]

Carissa and I seek out communities that align with the values that the Buddha highlighted. We go to a donation-based studio where yoga and meditation are generously offered regardless of one's ability to pay. When we see someone from the studio at the grocery store or biking down the street, it's an instant reminder of our shared connection around the values of generosity and spiritual development. This connection also helps the city feel like a small neighborhood.

Carissa: *Other ways that we find community in the city include greeting people in the stairwell or on the elevator—this is a very small form of generosity and community-building. Strangers often react in a lighthearted or humorous tone to whatever bit of conversation we start, because a small burden— awkwardness—has been lifted. What we say matters much less than the fact that we're acknowledging another person's presence and connecting on the level of our common humanity. We've made close friends in our building just by starting up a conversation about our WNBA team, the Minnesota Lynx. Had we avoided eye contact when we passed each other in the hall, we might still be strangers.*

In the wake of the increased national discrimination against so many communities (including indigenous peoples, immigrants, people of color, Muslims, women, and the LGBTQ community), a multitude of groups has been forming in Minneapolis. One of our relatives recently formed a group to get together on a monthly basis to organize grassroots events and activities to counteract this recent wave of discrimination. Making calls to representatives, mobilizing local communities, and going to marches, vigils, and protests are ways to take meaningful action based upon the wisdom and recognition that life is interconnected—hatred, discrimination, oppression, violence, and intolerance cause harm to all of us (not just those being targeted).

Taking action is also a way to live an engaged ethical commitment that supports service to others, stewardship, inclusivity, cooperation through trust, and belonging, which are part of a community-based expression of the five ethical precepts. It's also critically important and an expression of inner wisdom to take time to receive support from the community as a collective, especially when mental and physical stamina are needed to take action over weeks, months, and years. A dear friend of ours has convened a support meeting around the intersection of social justice and healing, where everyone in the group collectively processes the shock, disorientation, outrage, terror, and grief of various events so that we can continue to effectively respond and take action to what is needed. Without taking time to intentionally receive support from a wise community, despair and hopelessness are likely to occur.

Discipline and routine

It's no mistake that the Buddha's teaching includes an entire category on discipline. In fact, the Buddha's teachings are spoken of in terms of doctrine (*dharma*) and discipline (*vinaya*). Discipline is needed for progress on the spiritual path. In fact, the Buddha describes how starting with discipline, one eventually arrives at the highest freedom. [Pv XII.2]

Carissa and I have also found that routines and discipline, ironically, give a structure that provides greater freedom. We have a morning routine that provides us with a start to our workday. The alarm goes off around 5:30, and we go down to the small gym in our apartment building to work out. One of us showers while the other makes the morning breakfast. After getting ready, we meditate before enjoying our breakfast and heading out the door. This means that by the time we get to work, we've already taken care of our health—physically, nutritionally, and meditatively. It's a good start to the day that puts us in a positive mental state and ensures that regular meditation practice is a daily routine (which requires less effort and energy to sustain).

Carissa: *I have also experienced the power of routines within my kindergarten classroom over the years. By teaching the kids to follow certain routines—closing the door quietly when entering the room, walking instead of running, putting all materials back in their labeled place—I prepared them to have "Free Time" on Fridays, where they could choose from almost any activity in the classroom. Because they knew how to get along with one another, and respect the room and its materials, they were able to have the freedom to color, do puzzles, use the computers, or play with blocks. Students talked about "Free Time" all week leading up to Friday afternoons. The irony of this free time is that it wouldn't have been possible without the self-discipline that they had learned from the structures of the classroom environment, which came from the use of a daily routine. Free time was actually very orderly; it was not a free-for-all at all.*

As we make the final edits to this chapter, we both laugh as we read about our daily routines and how we seemingly have it all together. Our daughter was supposed to be born a week from today; she was born four weeks ago already. Having a premature baby who is spending her first month of life in the Neonatal Intensive Care Unit (NICU) is enough to keep anyone from going to the gym at 5:30 a.m. Not to mention that the majority of our summer has been spent at the hospital, so spending any time at home has been a huge challenge.

The question for us has been—in this temporary state of upheaval, and not knowing how long it will last—can discipline and routine still offer a path to greater freedom with what is happening?

The key insight for us over this past month in the hospital has been to find very concrete and simple activities that can be repeated on a daily basis to help intentionally connect us with states of well-being (versus the prudent and medically important assume-anything-might-go-wrong mindset of the hospital, which can be easily exacerbated in our minds as first-time parents). On most days, we manage to wander outside the hospital and sit on a park bench by the Mississippi River for ten minutes—a timer helps us to stay put and meditate or enjoy watching the ripples of the wind skimming the surface of the river below us. Instead of busing to work, I walk from the hospital to my office so that I can practice some informal walking meditation. Carissa takes at least fifteen minutes a day to find some solitude to journal and quietly drink a cup of coffee, clear her mind, and boost her spirits. We have both found that being intentional about celebrating each small accomplishment, like getting news of our daughter's stable glucose levels, is another simple structure that provides greater peace and supports well-being.

In addition to the support and love that we have felt from our own family and friends, we have come to feel a deep connection with the NICU community of nurses, doctors, social workers, chaplains, and other staff. Knowing that we can share our tears and joy with this community brings us strength, hope, and belonging during one of the most challenging periods of our life (so far).

These answers aren't perfect and it's always practice, but it's amazing to see how we can rely upon a discipline, which is now largely second nature, to help provide greater freedom and ease during difficult times. Like a newborn baby who needs to be swaddled in an open crib so that she can feel safe, developing a gentle discipline of practice within the rush of life can lead to an inner well-being that is embodied, adaptable, and sustainable.

Letting go . . .

Back on Hennepin Avenue, having missed the bus that would have gotten me to my 8 a.m. meeting, I find myself standing still in -8°F weather.

I feel the cracked skin on my hands—dried out from the lack of moisture in the air.

I see the salt-caked sidewalks splattered with spirals of white and brown.

I hear the sounds of jackhammers, bulldozers, construction cranes, and the methodical beep of a truck in reverse.

The warmth of the sun shines through a crystal-clear sky brought on by the extremely cold weather that has removed almost all the particles in the air.

I smile . . . I may have missed the bus; so what? I am happy right now and I am sure there's another bus not far behind.

PRACTICE IN THE MIDST OF ACTION

by Wildecy de Fatima Jury

For the last four years I have been nomadic, living between Oakland in California, Brooklyn in New York, and a municipal city called Anápolis, located a few hours from Brasilia in Brazil. In all these places, I basically practice the same way: sitting, breathing, and being aware of the sounds and smells, and sending *metta,* lovingkindness, to the world.

Each of these places presents a variety of unique elements that create challenges for me to concentrate and meditate regularly. However, these same elements when contemplated with awareness can greatly facilitate the ability to concentrate and meditate with tranquility. This awareness opens the doors to spiritual growth and to routinely cultivating certain meditation practices.

The four postures, *iriyapatha,* often mentioned in the Buddhist texts are walking, standing, sitting, and lying down. For me, the best way to practice stillness and become completely serene has been to sit on the cushion for a couple of hours each day and practice *anapanasati,* the mindfulness of breathing in and out. When I do sitting meditation, I am often able to calm my mind faster and reach a deeper level of concentration. I practiced as one of my teachers, Thanissara, said: *"To go beneath the place where we overly figure it out, overly think ourselves in this world, to receive within this deep receptive awareness that is listening, this present that can meet the body, the mind, the heart, the experiences that unfold."*

It has been while sitting on a *zafu* (meditation pillow) over a *zabuton* (meditation cushion) that I have experienced a type of stillness that offers some moments of liberation from preoccupation and avoidable suffering. Sitting on the cushion grounds me and helps me to reach a larger spaciousness where tenderness, acceptance, compassion, and forgiveness all dissolve into and align with the *dharma*. Sitting on the cushion also sharpens my ability to practice the mindfulness in the *Vipassana* Buddhism lineage when I stream from space to space. When it is not possible for me to sit on the cushion, I use other methods of practice.

In Oakland, there are a lot of distractions due to it being a major West Coast port city with various entertainments and social and political events. It is a busy and an exciting city where people from all over are moving in. The apartment where I live in Oakland is located on the back, on the second of four floors of a peach-colored building with sixteen apartments. Loud and unpleasant sounds appear continually or randomly, subsequently or simultaneously. Sounds of vacuum cleaners, blenders, hammers, loud TVs, and music are inside, and outside are seesaws, construction, and vehicles passing fast on the streets. And it appears that every half hour the sound of an airplane landing or taking off reverberates and shakes all the windows.

My olfactory senses, which have become more sensitive with time of practice, also offer a disruption. I am able to smell and name the type of food the neighbors are cooking and notice that these odors can be very unpleasant, particularly if they are of frying meat. Being a vegetarian and smelling an animal being cooked is extremely distasteful and a reason, according to my mind, to be judgmental and rancorous. So, the sounds and smells many times make it difficult for me to quiet my mind when meditating in Oakland.

Even with all these distractions, Oakland is where I have more chance to settle my mind to an astounding depth when I sit on the cushion. It is easier to be still in Oakland than in Brooklyn or Brazil. Why is that? Near the windows and almost touching the windows there is a tall, robust, contorted, brown tree. For some mystic reason its silhouette reminded me of a statue of Venus, the Roman goddess of love, on display at the British Museum that I saw in a magazine.

This ancient tree has a trunk with thousands of branches with stems and twigs spread all over, which create fascinating three-dimensional curved or perpendicular shapes: obliques, ovals, triangles, cylinders, spheres, circles. The immense blue sky is decorated with the greenish foliage and displayed through the open background of these shapes. Also, its trunk has thousands of fissures with distinctive colors, sizes, shapes, and textures. I think they are thousands of eyes looking at me when I meditate. These make-believe eyes evoke in me internally some manifestation of *Kwan Yin*, the goddess who hears all the cries of the world and looks at the world with compassion.

So, often before I sit to meditate, I contemplate this tree and its branches and fissures, and I create my *dharma* hall right there and make it a temple of "The Ten Thousand Buddhas" and *bodhisattvas* (beings who wish to attain enlightenment). Pretending that I am inside this temple, I feel as if I am in a retreat in a meditation center in the countryside. This contemplation is already the first step to soothing my mind.

I then pay attention to inhaling and exhaling and all senses. I meditate deliberately in this apartment where the sounds and smells that greatly annoyed me in the past no longer bother me. I am able to notice when the thoughts move to dimensions where pleasure and displeasure are absent. I am able to experience bare awareness easier because there, between the senses, is a type of quietness that allows me to reach a state of harmony and just perceive the notion of nothingness, of emptiness.

Another factor that makes it easier to quiet my mind in the busy city of Oakland, a boisterous location, is the support of the *sanghas* (communities of *dharma* practioners) that I belong to and can easily access, and where I meet regularly the kindhearted *kalyanamittas* (spiritual friendships), and the encouragement of many wise teachers who live and teach in the Bay Area.

I can meditate in Brooklyn, yet in Brooklyn it is more demanding and tiring to concentrate. The hindrances in Brooklyn are more poignant and hard to deal with. Many of the sounds in Brooklyn are similar to those in Oakland. But in Brooklyn there are more fire trucks, ambulances, and police sirens, and their alarm bells. There is more cursing and praising, and more loving or provoking loud voices, expressing either happiness or discontent. These distressing sounds suggest emergency and danger, which stir up strong feelings during meditating.

In Brooklyn, I still sit where there is a tree in front of the window. The tree is majestic and tall, with many branches, but not with the same particularity of Oakland's tree, my urban Ten Thousand Buddhas temple.

It took me several months to discipline myself to carry on my practice while in Brooklyn. I noticed that even sitting on a cushion did not work as well because the agitation that I was experiencing inside would not subside, either while or after I meditated. Also, no insights were arising to help me to comprehend what was happening in this new venue. Neither could I practice and inquire, nor could I reflect and change my mental formation patterns. I felt as if I was in a maze and in complete emotional upheaval. In other words, I was not able to sit still for even a short period of time and quiet my mind.

Then, suddenly, when I started to pay more attention to the specific conditionings that were increasing my suffering, I realized that I was having a strong reaction and aversion to what was happening in downtown Brooklyn. It was reported by *The New York Times* that the neighborhood where I was staying has the biggest economic disparity between the rich and the poor in the entire country. Gentrification, which is defined as the process of renewals and rebuilding accompanying the influx of middle-class or affluent people into deteriorating areas that often displaces poorer residents, was hurting me. I always felt sensitive to gentrification. But this time it seemed that the harm was more aggravated.

I realized then that I needed to explore that aching experience deeper in order to really understand what I needed to do. I started to walk around the neighborhood and to pay attention and observe this reality. And this reality is that on one side of the street where people of color live, primarily African Americans, Puerto Ricans, Dominicans, and some Asians, there are stigmas and stereotypes. This is one of the places where the complexity of poverty—its intersectional influences of crime, drug using and dealing, plus a high level of incarceration, and mental health issues—can be completely neglected and overlooked, and labeled laziness, and the strength and resilience of the residents can easily be invisible or dismissed.

On the other side of the street, the houses are being sold for millions or rented for inexcusable prices, mostly by young white people. The opulence of these new occupants is "berrante," in Portuguese, or gaudy. This situation perpetuates the incorrect assumption that we live in a society and an economic system that rewards hard work equally. This idea justifies gentrification and unequal development.

I realized that often when I walked around the neighborhood, I contemplated the changes and observed the racism and classism that mark these two realities. As a result, I many times noticed a feeling of hopelessness, of despair, of anger, and I noticed a constriction growing in my heart. Sitting on the cushion was not enough and was not freeing me. It was not until I started to practice more profound *mettā* and sending strong lovingkindness to everyone involved in this circumstance that I started to feel lighter, happier, compassionate, and accepting.

I have always practiced *metta*, but now this practice also had another facet. When sending *metta*, I included everyone who I think about or do not think about, everyone I see or don't see, everyone I talk to or do not talk to, everyone I hear or do not hear, everyone I feel or do not feel, and all visible and invisible beings. So, when I walked around, I looked at people that I knew I was sending *metta* to, so as to diminish the harm to them and to myself.

As I reflected more on the vigor of the *dharma*, on the intricacy of the human condition, and on the power of *shuniatta* (emptiness), my heart opened, and I stopped taking everything personally, generalizing, and directing my fury and disappointment towards a particular group of people. I reminded myself that, as much as I understood that there is work to do to change this paradigm, there are causes and conditions for this reality. I see that this reality is a continuation of collective *sankara*—pain and suffering, beliefs, opinions, tendencies—from ancestors, from the culture of my childhood and from a job where I worked for many years serving the disenfranchised people who are poor, immigrants, refugees, people of color in the US and from other countries. These communities, which have been facing colonization and subjugation for centuries, need lovingkindness as much as the oppressors, perpetrators, and predators need compassion. As Marlene Jones, a *dharma* teacher, wrote: "*The greatest teaching for me has been practicing compassion, first for myself, then for other individuals, and for all beings in all directions. It is here that I have found true freedom. Aché.*"

Besides sending *metta* to every sentient being, I started to chant daily and ring the bowl 108 times to purify the 108 *kilesas* (defilements) that some lineages of Buddhism believe all human beings carry inside. After cultivating *metta* more consciously, intentionally, and heartedly, I witnessed a fulfilling change in my meditation practice. It became easier to be present, to free my mind from noise or turbulence, and to experience peaceful states. I can say that in Brooklyn I was able to reach the first and second *jhanas* (meditative states or absorption) with less effort.

In Brazil I tried to maintain my sitting practice, to do *anapanasati* practice (the mindfulness of breathing in and out), to meditate noticing the sounds and smells, and to cultivate *mettā*. But in Brazil, there are also elements that make it difficult to still my mind, and there I more intentionally have had to cultivate the "practice in the midst of action"—actions that happen in society, and the deeply felt, life-changing actions that happen in the heart.

Mostly, I stay at my mother's home, a place that has always been very social. I belong to an extended family and I grew up in communities where people visit one another daily without making a phone call announcing they are coming to visit. So, the socialization in my mother's house is a lively continuation which I mostly greatly enjoy. However, it was initially very challenging for me to meditate. The noise from the streets, the peoples' voices early in the morning, and the TV's sound served as encumbrances that stopped me from meditating on a cushion. I noticed that I felt easily irritated, impatient, and uneasy, and I was having a very hard time practicing meditation either sitting on the cushion or any place else. I did then use earplugs when sitting.

When the earplugs did not work to help me to settle my mind, I walked to Praça Dom Emanuel, a busy public square near my mother's house, to practice meditating outside. In this square, there are several enormous, magnificent ficus trees that I sat under and just looked at their stillness and their shade, and enjoyed the freshness that they offered. From under these trees I could see the spaciousness of the sky, the beet colors of the ground, and the green vegetation in contrast with the orange-colored uniforms of the garis (street cleaners) lying on a bench resting during their lunch. I observed the smells of distinctive food. I also heard the assorted sounds—everyone speaking Portuguese; trucks with loudspeakers announcing a cultural event or a rally, the opening of a new store or gym, or that fruits and vegetables were for sale, or popsicles and ice cream, fresh cheese or *pamonhas* (a tamale-like dish), or tropical and savanna trees, or straw chairs, or Turkish rugs, or plastic weaved cord rugs; or the sound of the boom box and boom speakers in the cars passing by, or the hooves of the horses against the pavement, fireworks shooting, laughter, complaints, advice, children crying, people cursing and making plans and making jokes. And I felt the breeze refreshing me in a 40°C (104°F) day.

Observing all the senses, I cultivated being very present and just attuned to the sacredness of that moment. Even if it was just for a split second, that would be my meditation practice. In Brazil, I was able to expand my relationship with the distinct sounds and to widen my ability to be extremely present outside. The concept of being still and quieting my mind also stretched—to quiet the mind and be still is also to be totally alert to the moment, to the present.

There was also an event that happened in Brazil that gave me the chance to further deepen my practice "in the midst of action." Two years ago, my mother had a massive stroke. I immediately travelled there to be with her and my family and to help out. My siblings and I did not know if she was going to survive the stroke. She stayed in the hospital for a few weeks, and when she was brought home, she needed twenty-four-hour care.

I was one of the caretakers who bathed, fed, and took care of her hygiene. This was the first time I found myself directly facing the three universal fears: illness, aging, and death. No matter how prepared I and my siblings were, when my mother got sick we were in shock.

During that time, I used all the types of skills and support that I have acquired in California and Brooklyn to continue my practice and be present. I practiced mindfulness, awareness, compassion, and lovingkindness in everything I was doing, and in particular, when I was caring for my mother's basic needs and well-being. However, the fears, the confusion, the sadness, the grief, the anger for not accepting my mother's illness and vulnerability were overwhelming.

At first, I did not think about karma and causes and conditions and that her suffering was not only hers but it was also ours—a collective suffering. Then I realized that all of us who were witnessing her suffering were also experiencing a deep level of pain. I also noticed that to deal with the suffering I became very busy, efficient, and was doing everything very fast. By being fast I was avoiding being present. So, I would go back and forth without balance.

On one occasion, with a loving, humble, and gentle voice, my mother told me that sometimes my hands felt very heavy on her body. I slowed down at that moment but I noticed an unpleasant feeling permeating throughout my body. I became triggered and heard the old voices from childhood that told me I was unworthy. I became offended and self-righteous, and I wanted to contest, to defend myself, and to prove that that was not true. After a brief reflection and understanding the unhealthy pattern, I realized that being in a hurry was a way to deal with my mother's fragility.

Also, pitted against my mother's tenderness and the delicacy of that moment, I remembered that when I was a child, my mother, as a form of discipline, used often to hit me very hard. Even though my mother and I have had deep healing between us, past emotional wounds stored in my memory and in my body just appeared right there in my mind like in a flash. Perhaps unconsciously I was resentful, and therefore I was being rough.

Holding my tears, I started to breathe slowly and fully. I became totally present and aware that the unpleasant and unwholesome feelings were dissipating. This interaction with my mother offered me the opportunity to once more understand how dependent origination works in practice: "If this exists, that exists; if this ceases to exist, that also ceases to exist." The hurt from the past and its influence in my present life did not need to exist. I just detached from what did not need to exist anymore. Breathing in and out, with serenity, acceptance, and empathy, I assured my mother that I would pay attention, slow down, be more attentive, and be softer. She just said, Okay. My heart overflowed with love, tenderness, affection, and compassion.

After that interaction, when I was caring for my mother I frequently chanted or recited the *brahmaviharas*, and in particular the *metta* chant that says: *"May I accept my condition gracefully."* I also practiced the Thirty-Two Parts of the Body Meditation out loud in Portuguese with my mother, who repeated after me without hesitation or resistance. Because my mother is very Catholic, I respected her practice and prayed Catholic prayers, watched mass on TV, and went to the church with her as well.

And we laughed. I told her funny stories I knew about her growing up, her marriage, and about relatives and friends. I played harmonica and piano on the iPad for her and with her, and I taught her some phrases in English. Then I made videos of her doing all these activities and showed them to her. She laughed and was happy. All these actions became deliberately part of my daily meditation practice. That was a way to practice the

Eightfold Path daily as well: right aspiration, right view, right speech, right action, right livelihood, right effort, right mindfulness, and right concentration. I also practiced the *paramis* (qualities of the heart) of the generous giving of my time, of renunciation of any expectations, of patience by being present, of lovingkindness, and, when possible, equanimity.

To practice on the move, in the midst of action, is confusing, challenging, and demanding, but it is possible, and it is also gratifying, wholesome, and rewarding.

GOOD ENOUGH: LOVINGKINDNESS FOR SELF

by Eve Decker

"You can look the whole world over and find no one more deserving of your love than yourself."

—THE BUDDHA

I wave the electronic key at the sensor to the door of Oakland's Kehilla Community Synagogue. I'm buzzed in. I lug my guitar and backpack through the foyer and hall to the back classroom, filled with preschool memorabilia in Hebrew, plastic chairs, and tables. I have stored a rolled-up carpet in a closet; I pull that out and unroll it in the middle of the room. I unlock the back door and take the stairs down to my car in the parking lot, which is filled with tea supplies, pillows, blankets, a bag of clipboards and pens, and handouts for the class. I spend the next twenty minutes doing the best I can to transform the center of the syna- gogue classroom into a warm circle for meditation, reflection, sharing, and learning.

At about 6:45, the students begin to arrive. They have made their way from all around Oakland, and from neighboring cities as far as an hour and a half away. What brings them here? Their recognition that self-denigration—the language of self-hate—happens too much, too often, right there, silently, within their own heads. Each has left the comfort of their familiar routines to come tonight, to sing, learn, and practice techniques from the Buddhist tradition that grow self-acceptance, and thus well-being.

I grew up in a San Francisco suburb. An urban kid, growing up with glamour magazines, billboards, and TV shows. Like millions of other kids, I learned some things about what is required to belong in the "tribe" of mainstream Western culture: be fit, be wealthy, be extroverted. Women in this society (according to media stories teaching impressionable minds about culture) smile all the time, care-take, and are thin and sexy. They make perfect soufflés, have lots of energy, and succeed easily.

These messages benefit advertisers, but often have a very terrible consequence—few people can meet their criteria for belonging.

Not feeling a sense of belonging is a red flag to a hardwired part of the brain—that part that evolved towards fitting into the group in order to survive. Then, the prefrontal cortex spins stories to explain why we are not fitting in. My brain spun the story that I later learned is *epidemic* in the currently dominant Western culture: I'm the problem. I am not good enough. I will be chronically inadequate.

As people settle in to the class, we sing short repeating songs with words that remind us to breathe, to center, to relax. So many of us need to be reminded that we can feel what's actually happening here in the lived present moment, rather than filter it through the hyper-vigilance needed for a typical stressful urban day.

To fit in, to belong, my mind—like so many—created a fierce inner critic designed to keep me headed in the direction of belonging. "There's something wrong with you! You're not attractive enough! You're always in a rush! You're too fat! You're not doing it right! You're not working hard enough!" And it backfired. With a voice of self-contempt shouting in my mind, I actually became less connected with others and thus felt less belonging. So, I had unintentionally placed myself in the middle of a vicious circle: Less of a sense of belonging = more self-criticism. More self-criticism = less self-confidence. Less self-confidence = less connecting with others. Less connecting with others = less of a sense of belonging. . . . And on it went.

> *After singing and guided mindfulness practice, group members check in. Manuel is a young elementary school teacher from the south Bay Area. It takes him about three hours round trip on BART to come to the Lovingkindness-for-Self group. He speaks about his very critical father, and how difficult it has always been to feel a sense of belonging in his family when the bar has been set impossibly high.*
>
> *Jerri has a law degree and two children. She speaks of her despair and rage about not ever meeting the social criteria for attractiveness, and how aging is making that even harder.*

I made it to my late twenties before I finally admitted to myself that I was depressed—depressed by my inability to become what I wasn't. Because I was so identified with my inner critic, I thought the solution was to change who I was and eliminate the things about me that did not meet the standard offered by mainstream society. I could not see any alternative. And when my natural self proved to be stronger than my most profound intention to change it, I despaired. This type of despair is no joke. It's isolating and can lead to checking-out through addiction and other behaviors. My addiction (don't laugh, cuz this is a real thing—six to eight times more addictive than cocaine and lots of bad effects on the body) was sugar. I ate lots and lots of it in order to numb out my pain about not being the kind of person who seemed to belong.

Enter Buddhist practice. I went to my first meditation class at the Northbrae Community Church in Berkeley in 1991. James Baraz, who was and is a teacher at Spirit Rock Meditation Center in California, was teaching the fundamentals of mindfulness. I can't remember what he said that night, but I remember crying with relief. Here was a practice that might teach me how to not be at the mercy of my internalized cultural conditioning that talked to me as my own voice in my head.

There is a parable in Buddhism about different kinds of horses, and how they mimic different kinds of students. There is the fast horse, the regularly moving horse, and the slow horse. They all eventually get to their destination. I am a slow horse. I practiced mindfulness on retreats ranging from one day to three months for several years. It took me years of sitting on my cushion derailed by the thinking mind before I could stay with my direct experience of the rise and fall of breath in my abdomen. But I kept returning to the retreats, and kept up an at-home practice. In my apartment in Oakland, with the cars whizzing by outside, I would sit on my cushion or on a chair and practice letting go of my thoughts and feeling my abdomen rise and fall.

Victoria, a social justice activist, speaks about not having time for a regular meditation practice. Her challenge is echoed by most people in the room—how do we find time to strengthen our capacity for mindfulness when time is at such a premium? And yet a capacity for mindfulness— bringing the mind's awareness away from the stories it's telling and into the lived present moment—is an essential skill for disengaging from negative thinking. Together, we generate strategies to support the crucial practice of daily meditation. Begin by making the commitment short enough to be possible (some people have a three-minute daily practice to start). Use group members as buddies for accountability. Have a time and place for practice that can become habituated. Learn that sound from the environment and stress from daily life are not obstacles to meditation—they can be a part of it, by just bringing our awareness to them.

Every little break that I got from the dense lattice of thoughts was a tiny drop of freedom. You may have heard that you are not your thoughts, but that's a hard concept to understand until you experience it directly. Even a few moments of living without concepts, just pointing the mind's awareness to the direct experience of the present moment, builds up over time. More and more I was able to get some distance from my thoughts and see that many of them were habitual, but they weren't me.

But who was I then, if not the hopeless mess my inner critic judged me to be?

What I observed about myself during extended periods of mindfulness practice—and quickly saw was true of others as well—was that I am generally good, though imperfect. Although I was already a basically ethical and generous person, I needed some different inner self talk, so that the inner critic didn't always have the floor, making mountains out of the molehills of my imperfections. After about ten years of practicing mindfulness, when it had become habituated, I added a lovingkindness practice.

The energy of lovingkindness is one of gentle befriending. Lovingkindness practice is silently saying well-wishing phrases—offering them to yourself or others. One version of the traditional phrases goes like this: "May you be safe, may you be happy, may you be healthy, may you live with ease." Once I had managed to somewhat dis-identify from toxic conditioned thought, I needed something that would not upset my system to take its place. In a garden, that would look like flowers replacing weeds. Lovingkindness phrases can be great for that—a friendly voice in the head rather than a criticizing one.

> *"Research shows that positive, reassuring messages create the mind-state most conducive to working hard and reaching our potential. We need to feel calm, secure, and confident to do our best."*
> —Kristen Neff, PhD, *Self-Compassion*

> *"I practice my lovingkindness phrases while I drive," shares Tai. "I don't do the 'May I,' I just chant to myself: 'Let there be love.' Usually I have a lot of road rage, but it's harder to get pissed off when I'm hearing 'Let there be love' in my head."*

What I discovered after practicing lovingkindness phrases for a while was that I could authentically offer well wishes for others—but I didn't believe myself when I sent them towards myself. They seemed fake and uncomfortable and I also felt embarrassed—they seemed self-aggrandizing. "May I be safe, may I be happy, may I be healthy, may I live with ease"—was hard for me to take in.

When I spoke about this with a Buddhist teacher, he suggested that I spend all of the time I was allotting for practice—both mindfulness and lovingkindness—saying the lovingkindness phrases to myself.

My "aha" moment came one evening on a meditation retreat, listening to the sound of frogs in the creek outside. I felt strong, uncomplicated love for the frogs. And then I wondered, "Why am I believing that the frogs are worthy of my love but I am not? Why are the frogs better than me?" I realized that, like the frogs, I am made by the universe. My value comes in part from being a miracle of the cosmos, like the frogs. My essence is peaceful and kind, and when I listen to and act from that part of myself, my access to self-acceptance increases. My body, like the frogs', is made of the elements of earth, and I am sustained and held by this earth. I am worthy of my own care as all beings are worthy of care.

Now, for you reading this, the above may seem obvious. But trust me when I say there is a huge contingent of people out there who, like me, just couldn't find our inherent worthiness through the thick fog of the conditioned, thinking mind.

I returned from that retreat having had a warm, amazing experience being able to hold myself in love. My imperfections were just as clear as before, but instead of being reasons for the inner critic to kick me in the shins, they just included me as a part of the family of living things. But how to sustain that insight born of silence, lovingkindness practice, and frogs once I was back in the East Bay?

I looked around at my fellow travelers in the city, human and animal. Nothing, and no one, is perfect. And all, like me, like the frogs, are a part of the cosmos, trying to do our best with what we have learned, assumed, and been given. Really understanding that truth and not fighting it, but rather cultivating patience and compassion—for all beings, including myself—is a part of the road to self-love.

Ella speaks about trouble with her son, and her habit of self-blame around her parenting when her son has difficult behaviors. She tells the group what was different this time: she recalled and used mindfulness to stop her ruminative thinking, and then employed strategies of self-compassion, patience, and lovingkindness to bring some balance and perspective before addressing her son's issue. Her response to both her son and herself felt wiser and calmer. She noticed that her self-esteem stayed intact.

"Those who truly love themselves could never harm another."

—The Buddha

I see, with a heart of compassion, that we are pretty much at the mercy of our conditioning—believing what we think, and thinking what we've learned or assumed—until we have developed practices that counter that conditioning.

As I myself have gotten more and more freed from what I think of as "inner colonization"—the toxic trance of mainstream Western culture (some of us send this stuff outward, some, like me, apply it inward, and some do both)—I have identified several key practices from Buddhism that support long-term freedom from self-directed hatred. I wrote them up into a curriculum, along with songs and poetry that support them. These classes have been filling up for the three years I've been teaching them—evidence that we need new ways to find inner peace, and the Buddha's teachings from almost 2,600 years ago can provide some of these "new"/ancient paths to peace.

We close our class with a sung Dedication of Merit. The "Dedication of Merit" is a Buddhist tradition offering the "merit" or good energy generated from genuine efforts to transform suffering to all beings. Together we sing, "May all become compassionate and wise."

Freed from identification with conditioned thought, and supported by the practice of lovingkindness, almost all people and animals are clearly precious now, as the frogs were to me that night long ago. Loved ones, imperfect too, are precious. All the millions of neutral beings—people driving in the freeway traffic, people hanging out on the street corners, dogs on leashes or at the shelter, grocery clerks, crows, kids, elders—all precious. The Buddha taught that even the *difficult* beings are precious, worthy of our care.

This can be directly experienced once we've teased apart our own essence (good) from much of our (often not so good) cultural conditioning. And with this insight, as poet Naomi Shihab Nye put it, *"Only kindness makes sense anymore."* We come to see what the Buddha taught is true: *"One who truly loves themselves would never harm another."* Freed from limiting beliefs about ourselves, the miraculous tender shimmer of all beings becomes apparent.

May *all beings* be free. Free from suffering, and free from the delusion of "not good enough."

A STRANGER IN THE CITY: LESSONS FROM TRAVELING

by Alice Alldredge

I don't live in a big city. My town has no subways, intra-city trains, street-cars, or metros. So, finding my way into and around a new city by public transportation can be daunting. Attempting to navigate a new transportation system while surrounded by crowds of people walking at breakneck speed, who all seem to know exactly where they are going, has been a sure recipe for confusion, doubt, and frustration. But it has also offered wonderful opportunities to deepen my practice. Here are some of my favorite lessons.

Waiting for the train—Perception

A few years ago, my husband and I took a much-anticipated trip to Europe. We were to land in Frankfurt and take a train from Frankfurt up the Rhine Valley to the small village of Bacharach where we would spend a few nights. I had carefully researched how to make the connections by train. We had to take one train out of Frankfurt and then transfer to a second train in a large city down the line. We got to the transfer station about 10 o'clock at night and went out to the platform to wait, exhausted, jet-lagged, and numb from our long flight. A train with a few cars was sitting on a spur next to the backside of the platform, but the number on the engine was not our number. That couldn't be our train. Our train with the correct number would come down the main track soon. Finally, a train did arrive on the main line and several groups of people got off and got onto the train waiting on the spur. At my husband's urging, I asked one of them if the train went to Bacharach, but that passenger had never heard of it.

It was getting close to the time for us to depart. Where was our train? And where were all the other people who should be waiting on the platform to get on it? We were all alone on the platform when the train on the spur pulled out, and the lighted sign above the platform and entire platform went dark. I was filled with a terrible sinking feeling. The train on the spur had been our train all along and it was leaving! But the number on the engine was the wrong number. How could that be? We were so exhausted and that was the last train! My husband's gray, downcast face said it all. He was too tired even to be upset. I took him by the hand and led him out to the front of the train station where we found a cab willing to drive us the sixty miles to Bacharach.

What a lesson in the power of perception. I was so sure our train would come down the main track with the right engine number. There was absolutely no doubt in my mind about these facts. I was unable to see any other possibilities. I was so certain that I never even considered asking at the ticket window for more information. My incorrect perception left us stranded and dejected there in the dark on the platform. Mark Twain said it best: *"It ain't what you don't know that gets you into trouble. It's what you know for sure that just ain't so."*

This experience is such a metaphor for the power of perception in our lives. How many opportunities have I passed up to meet fascinating and insightful people because my perception of their clothes, hairstyle, accent, tattoos, gender, or skin color led me to label them as uninteresting, ignorant, hostile, or dangerous? How many potentially enlightening experiences have I missed because I misperceived them as perilous, risky, worthless, or boring?

Perception is that mental process that picks out the distinguishing characteristics of an object, idea, or experience, compares it against similar characteristics in our memory, and then recognizes and names it. We hear a chirping sound. Our mind compares it with other similar sounds we have heard in the past and identifies it as a bird. I see a number on the side of a train, compare it to my understanding of how train systems work, and identify it as the wrong train.

Perception is absolutely essential for our existence. It's a fundamental faculty of the minds of all animals. Without it we would not be able to function or survive. We need to be able to identify and label the objects in our environment in order to make sense of the world and navigate it with safety and success. If our tribal ancestors had not been able to perceive a certain color and movement in the grass as a lion, we would not be here today. If I can't perceive the dark object moving toward me in the intersection as a car, I am likely to be run over. We are able to communicate and interact because we share common perceptions. If I ask you for a pan to cook the eggs, you know what I mean because we share a common perception of what is a pan, an egg, and the process of cooking.

But the problem with perception is that it simplifies complex real phenomena into concepts. And those concepts can imprison us by keeping us from seeing the true nature of our experience. For example, many of our experiences are combinations of many perceptions that we collapse down into a single feeling. As someone not used to the hustle and bustle of a large city, I have occasionally found that the cacophony of blaring horns, sirens, car engines, and human voices coupled with the rush of many pedestrians walking rapidly around me on the sidewalk can generate a perception of chaos or danger. I feel overwhelmed and vulnerable. Yet, if I focus on the individual experiences making up my perception, I immediately calm down. There is nothing threatening about a car in the distance or a particular person walking past me. With mindfulness, these separate perceptions become manageable. It is only when my mind combines them into a single concept of chaos that they may seem unbearable.

In labeling our experience, we lose touch with the complexity and the reality of what we are seeing. The beautiful, lyrical sound we hear is less intimate and less immediate when our mind slaps the concept of a bird onto it. Looking out into a city park, our eyes only register color, light, and shadow. It is our mind that turns those into the concept of a tree.

Just as a tree is a composite of many things, the experiences on a city sidewalk are a composite of many perceptions. A tree is composed of bark, branches, and leaves, each made of even smaller components. Labeling it as a "tree" reduces our ability to perceive its complexity. We see it as a single solid thing and lose insight into its true nature. Because we perceive only its surface appearance, our experience loses some of its potential richness.

But most important of all, concepts cause us to perceive what is impermanent as permanent. The "tree" in the park is changing every moment. The sap is flowing throughout, cells are dividing, leaves are dying and dropping, and new leaves are being added. The tree is changing shape before our eyes. What we call a tree is not a noun at all. It's a verb. In fact, everything in our experience is changing all the time. There are no nouns. Everything is a verb. It's just that some verbs are so slow that we perceive them as solid objects. We perceive a passing cab on the street as a permanent object but it too is changing every moment. It's just changing quite slowly. Gas is being burned, each passenger rubs molecules off the seat covers, and the body of the cab is oxidizing and slowly rusting. If we were to see the same cab ten years in the future it will have become worn and dilapidated. The changes that we can't see over short spans of days would become obvious to us over a span of years. Yet, by labeling these objects with the concept of "tree" or "cab," they become permanent in our minds. We do not perceive their changing nature. We misperceive them as solid objects rather than as ever-changing processes.

When we misperceive what is impermanent as permanent, we set ourselves up for suffering. The cab wears out, our precious vase cracks, our computer breaks down, our beloved friend dies, and our own bodies wither with age. These changes are inevitable, but we resist them with all our hearts. We grieve our losses and bemoan the unfairness of life. It is only when we begin to see through our perception of permanency that we can fully grasp the deeper truth of reality that nothing is permanent. Deeply accepting that everything is in a process of change can bring us a great sense of balance and peace. We are better able to navigate the losses and gains, and the pleasures and pains of life. We learn to accept these vicissitudes with grace and wisdom.

The memory of missing the train in Europe has become a poignant reminder to examine my perceptions. That examination is particularly helpful when strong afflictive emotions or mind states arise. How do I perceive an experience that leads me to feel vulnerable, judgmental, fearful, angry, self-righteous, or sad? Is my perception correct or is it based on stories I might be telling myself? Deeply examining our perceptions is an important part of the path to tranquility and peace, no matter what our surroundings. It can help lead us to that inner stillness even in the midst of a busy city.

Getting on the wrong bus—Equanimity

Navigating a new city also presents many opportunities to practice equanimity. During our trip to Europe, my husband and I were in eastern

Berlin waiting to catch a city bus to the airport. Impulsively, my husband just jumped onto the first bus that came along. But it was the wrong bus. Standing there on the curb, I could feel a series of painful emotions arise, including panic, dismay, frustration, and anger. I quickly hopped onto the bus, too, since I did not want us to be separated.

As we approached the next stop, I asked myself *"What would be the worst thing that could happen here?"* I have found this question to be so useful in helping me find equanimity and calm. We might miss the plane. Would that be the end of the world? No. We would certainly get home somehow. We could also catch a cab to the airport when we got off this bus. So, the worst thing might be a little extra expense. I felt calm return. We got off at the next stop, caught a bus back to the original stop, and waited for the correct bus. My husband was chagrinned and embarrassed. We laughed about it together and made the plane on time.

When I find myself thrown off balance, the answer to the question *"What would be the worst thing that could happen here?"* is often so trivial and unimportant that I end up laughing at the workings of my own mind. That feeling of anxiety that develops when I am running late for an appointment subsides when I realize that the worst thing that could happen would be my embarrassment at slipping in late, or that I might miss the first few minutes of a movie, or that the restaurant might not hold the table. The consequences of being late are often small, yet the feelings of pressure to be on time can become overwhelming. So often we get an idea in our mind, like the idea that we can't be late, and then we cling to it so tenaciously that it causes us considerable angst and discomfort. We believe the thought and give it a reality of its own.

The Buddha was very clear about the Second Noble Truth. Clinging is the cause of suffering. Equanimity can be reestablished by challenging the validity of our thoughts and by examining the underlying assumptions that we hold. This loosens our grasping at an idea that is causing us suffering and opens us to the possibility of freedom in this moment.

Getting off the bus—Trust

In Siena, Italy, my husband and I boarded a city bus going toward the outskirts of the city, where we would rent a car for a few days. The bus was full of Italians commuting from work, so I was standing in the aisle. I could not see any of the street signs from where I stood. The bus wound around for a long time through a variety of commercial and residential districts. I realized I had no idea where our stop was on the route. I could feel a sense of panic, confusion, and anxiety rising up as tightness in my belly and chest.

And then the thought arose that I was safe in that moment. The bus would make its loop again if we missed the stop. It wasn't a big deal. The panic subsided and a sense of calm and equanimity replaced it. Everything would be OK. At that point I was composed enough to see the situation clearly and to decide what to do. I could not reach the bus driver, so I simply turned to the middle-aged Italian woman standing next to me and asked:

"Do you speak English?"

"Of course!" she answered adamantly, with surprise that I would even need to ask. Then she helped us find the correct stop.

Even if she hadn't spoken English, she spoke the common human language of compassion and concern for others, and she would have found a way to help us. Moreover, she was not alone on the bus in this regard. My husband was distracted and left his backpack on the bus seat as he got off. Four people jumped up to call him back and hand it to him.

Navigating big cities has offered many lessons regarding this basic human capacity for connection. Kindness is in abundance everywhere I have traveled. I can't remember how many times I have pulled out a map on the sidewalk of a large city and within a couple of minutes had someone approach me to ask if they could help me find my way.

I visited New York City for the first time recently. In a city with a reputation for abruptness and reserve, everyone I stopped to ask directions was helpful, open, welcoming, and even eager to share their pride in their great city. But the kindness went farther than just friendliness. It extended to true generosity and openheartedness. I was having difficulty learning how to obtain a reusable subway pass from a machine at a metro entrance my first day in New York. The woman in line behind me thought the machine was broken. She took me over to another machine, checked to be sure it was working, gave me her own spare pass to keep, and helped me learn how to put money onto it. She was so gracious, patient, and generous, both with her time and her pass. We knew each other for only a few minutes but felt like old friends when we parted.

A day later, I watched a couple from China, tourists with little English, get onto a city bus. But their bus passes had expired and they did not have the exact change needed for boarding. As they began to get off the bus a passenger near the front jumped out of her seat and paid their fare. It was such a simple act of kindness, but one that left all who saw it with a glow in our hearts and a smile on our faces.

As a visitor in a new city, I have learned to trust in this basic goodness of strangers. I can only imagine how many countless millions of strangers help each other every day on this planet. My faith that Buddha nature exists in all of us has been greatly strengthened by my experiences in cities. We all have within us the capacity to develop the pure, luminous mind of a Buddha, a mind filled with compassion and wisdom. It is only our fears, desires, and delusions that conceal this capacity. They are like clouds that obscure our true nature. When we reach out to help someone, those clouds part a little. Our compassion shines forth and we feel connected, kind-hearted, and enriched in some inexplicable way. As Lydia Child has said, *"An effort made for the happiness of others lifts us above ourselves."* Whenever I have approached a stranger for help in a friendly and open way, I have almost always been rewarded by a response that enhances our sense of connection to our common humanity. In a few cases that connection has even blossomed into a continuing friendship.

Connecting it all—Mindfulness

There is a sense of freedom in traveling—a sense of excitement, adventure, and freshness as we anticipate each new experience—that makes mindfulness arise naturally. We easily gravitate to our present moment experience because its novelty becomes so compelling and absorbing. We are less likely to fall back into ruminations and become lost in thought. But as I contemplate the lessons I have learned from visiting cities, I realize that the most important aspect of mindfulness has been the monitoring of my own internal reactions to my experience. Noticing the arising of confusion, doubt, disquiet, and frustration, as well as delight, has been essential in helping me restore calm within the rush and turmoil of a busy city. The still center, the place of tranquility and equanimity, is always within our own hearts, no matter where we are. Even in the midst of seeming chaos and potential overwhelm we can find peace and stability within. Taking a mindful breath or a moment to pause can bring us back to center, reconnect us with our bare experience, and reveal the insight needed to move forward. Although we may be a stranger in the city, that still point remains a place of familiarity and safety, a refuge always available to us.

DHARMA, TRUTH

CLEARLY KNOWING IN NEW YORK

by nakawe cuebas

Bahiya Sutta:

   In the seen, there is only the seen.
   In the heard, there is only the heard.
   In the sensed (smell, taste, and touch),
    there is only the sensed.
   In the cognized, there is only the cognized.
   This, Bahiya, is how you should train yourself.
   When, Bahiya, there is for you,
   In the seen only the seen,
   In the heard only the heard,
   In the sensed only the sensed,
   In the cognized only the cognized.
   Then, Bahiya, there is no "you"
   In connection with all that.
   When, Bahiya, there is no "you"
   In connection with all that,
   There is no "you" there.
   When, Bahiya, there is no "you" there,
   Then, Bahiya, you are neither here

Nor there,

Nor in between the two.

This, just this, is the end of suffering.

Embodied presence with clear comprehension allows wisdom to unfold. Exploring mindfulness in the city can be quite a challenging training. So, my practice has been and continues to be, anywhere, anytime, staying present both internally and externally with whatever is arising with an open heart and mind, and when I close up my heart and mind, seeing that too. This is where the Buddha was directing us in the *Satipatthana Sutta.*

Can I stay internally present, mindful, and perhaps even peaceful and openhearted, as my senses are bombarded with the sights, sounds, and smells of the city? Can I find places in the city for some external space and stillness? The answer to both questions is yes.

I have noticed that over sixty-three years of growing up and living in New York, as my meditative practice deepened, peace in heart and mind have deepened, and I have been able to be more at ease with whatever is happening in the city, no matter how loud the noise, how annoying the crowds.

As in the instructions given by the Buddha to Bahiya, quoted above— in the seen, there is only the seen; in the heard, there is only the heard; in the sensed, there is only the sensed; in the cognized, there is only the cognized—the bare, simple, direct awareness of what's coming into our experience. So, I start there.

Walking in the Big Apple, there are times when I can choose extremely crowded and busy streets to walk. A walk down 42nd Street to the Signature Theatre to meet friends is an onslaught of lights and glitter, the loud sounds of traffic, an experience of massive numbers of beings all around, talking and laughing, odors of food vendors. And then there is "me"—embodied presence—aware of walking, feeling legs moving, feet stepping, body in motion, weaving around bodies in space, very little space at that, present with all as it is. Being aware when mind wanders into thinking, bringing awareness back into body and into mind uncluttered with judgments, opinions, stories—wonderful practice. Walking the street and radiating *metta* (lovingkindness). Sending well wishes brings the warmth to my heart and to the hearts of fellow beings walking this planet, as we all search for happiness and well-being. Sometimes I choose quieter streets; perhaps I walk to the theater around the back on 41st Street where there is a little bit less of the above.

Or, I walk among the West Side streets lined with beautiful brownstones and trees. In the summer, there are flower boxes in the windows and flowers by the doorways. Again, embodied presence—walking, feeling legs moving, feet stepping, body in motion, my breath moving in and out of this body, present with all as it is, keeping the heart open and free.

When I'm mindful, I'm seeing what is coming in through my internal world and external world with bare awareness. But, according to the *Satipatthana*, mindfulness (*sati*) operates in combination with clear comprehension (*sampajana*). This is where wisdom is cultivated. Clear comprehension is the lens for seeing what's skillful or unskillful; it is the "illuminating" or "awakening" aspect of contemplation. And, what we see clearly is that all things that arise will pass away, all things are not self, and when we cling and grasp through craving and desire we suffer.

With all the passing sensations of the city that arise in my mind or my mind in relationship to the outside world, whether pleasant or unpleasant, I can let nature be and let it go. I can savor the pleasant, even knowing it's built in impermanence; I can be present with the unpleasant, knowing it's changing even as it's happening—"this too shall pass."

When we keep mind and heart uncluttered, then we can be really present and not let life pass by unnoticed.

So, I am riding on a crowded, noisy subway car, someone gets up to leave and I take the seat. The lady next to me comments on how lovely my green bag is. I tell her it's a gift from a dear friend. We proceed into a conversation on this crowded subway car, two spirits connecting, conversing as old friends, although we just met—openhearted. We part paths, each going on our way—very pleasant, very impermanent, touching that deep place of connection with all beings.

Then, I am walking down the street during lunch break from my job in the Bronx. I heard on the news this morning that someone got shot at the deli on the next block. I see blood on the sidewalk; my heart aches for the tragedy, for both the victim and the perpetrator. I take a deep breath and send *metta* and compassion to both—for the suffering, for impermanence, for a mind filled with fear, hatred, and confusion—touching that deep place of connection with all beings.

And, finally, I look up to the vast limitless sky as a constant reminder of the true empty nature of everything.

Some of my favorite meditative spots in the city offer that view. And I can now go back to the second question. Can I find places in the city for some external space and stillness? The answer is yes!

Of course, Central Park is a favorite. When I lived on 110th Street, I only had to cross the street to enter the park and would sit by the beautiful pond and take in the trees, water, stillness amidst the sounds of the city, children playing, the birds singing, the traffic hum. The Conservatory Garden at Fifth Avenue between 104th and 105th Streets is an oasis of beautiful flowers and plants—a peaceful place to sit and enjoy the shade and blooms.

But I have also spent many beautiful moments on Orchard Beach in the Bronx, both alone and with a dear friend. We even sat through a snowstorm there, a truly amazing experience. On a midweek day, no traffic, quietude, sand, Long Island Sound waters.

I don't advise swimming there, however! But if you're like me, truly a mermaid in disguise, you will find beaches for swimming. Brooklyn has beaches.

And, while growing up, I spent many a family outing a short distance outside of the city on Long Island at Jones Beach. Really quite beautiful. And, yes, you can swim there in the midst of the wonderful waves. Being Puerto Rican, my family would cook loads of food. Ecstasy for me was water, swimming, delicious home-cooked food, and cousins to play the day away with. Those are beautiful memories, and when I visit now alone or with friends, yes, I can be mindful there too.

When I lived in the Bronx, I used to sit by a small pond in Woodlawn Cemetery, a really beautiful cemetery. It is very peaceful there. I was surrounded and touched by the creative cosmic ancestral juices of some really cool people buried at Woodlawn: Queen of Salsa Celia Cruz; jazz musicians Miles Davis, Lionel Hampton, and Milt Jackson, among others.

Sitting there amidst beings that once had lived on this earth, lives lived filled with all the ten thousand joys and ten thousand sorrows we all go through, and now gone, separated from all they knew on this earth, I am deeply reminded that this body too is impermanent, and will come to an end, I know not when.

So you should view this fleeting world,
A star at dawn, a bubble in a stream,
A flash of lightening in a summer cloud,
A flickering lamp, a phantom, and a dream
                                        —THE DIAMOND SUTTA

So, taking a deep breath, I come back to this precious moment where true freedom is always possible with an awakened heart and mind, with gratitude in my heart for these amazing teachings, taking refuge in the Buddha, the *Dhamma*, and the *Sangha*.

The journey continues . . .

IMPERMANENCE

by Tracy Cochran

"In three words I can sum up everything I've learned about life. It goes on," writes Robert Frost.

In three words I can sum up the aim of mindfulness meditation. Being with change.

"See that sign for the David Barton Gym?" asked the woman walking ahead of me on Sixth Avenue in Manhattan, addressing the teenagers walking on each side of her. She gestured to an old stone church on the corner of West 20th Street. *"What a sacrilege."* The group of us stopped together for a moment, waiting for the light to change. *"This was The Limelight. It was a famous nightclub. I used to come here all the time."* The light turned green and the kids surged ahead without giving the church a glance. I guessed they were her children because they were benignly indifferent. Her nightclub days were clearly behind her. I turned left to go the *Parabola* office and they walked on.

What seemed a sacrilege to her, I thought, was the passing of a place of memories that were vivid and deep. Once I had the chance to ask Zen Master Thich Nhat Hanh why people seem to cling to their suffering, defining themselves by it. People cling to their strongest impressions, he told me. Then and there, I realized the art of life had to do with making good impressions, moments of feeling peaceful and safe and open to life, as alluring and powerful as painful impressions. I pictured the woman on

75

the street twenty years ago, dancing at The Limelight, feeling anything seemed possible. Maybe she had been in love. The trick is that the more sublime something is, the more painful it can be when it goes.

Today, the church that was formerly The Limelight is not just a gym but also Grimaldi's pizza, a warren of expensive little shops, and the upscale Chinese restaurant Jue Lan. The Limelight nightclub was shut down for drug-selling in 1995. What a sacrilege it seemed to people then, turning a house of prayer into a gigantic den of drugs and debauchery.

Once I went to a lavish party there, thrown by the publisher of a magazine I wrote for. I remember wandering through dark and cavernous rooms, marveling that a place of stillness and the sacred was now full of music and bars and hipster children. The publisher host wore a tuxedo and a smug smile. Dark and gleaming, surrounded by dry ice fog, he looked like a New York Caligula. I wondered if being invited to the party meant that I was getting somewhere, but it felt like I was a little speck in the storm. Now he and the magazine and the club and its air of hell and my reactions to it are all gone, giving way to new life. Nothing stays the same.

The Buddha taught that the existence of all ordinary sentient beings is marked by impermanence. Change is constant everywhere, but New York City is a particularly easy place to observe it. The night of the party at The Limelight, I lived in an artsy neighborhood in the East Village. After I married and my daughter was born, I moved to a big apartment with soaring ceilings in a mostly Italian neighborhood that was beginning to see an influx of artsy young people. In the blink of an eye, that neighborhood was chic and very expensive. Two members of the Gambino family who owned the building we rented came and told us that it was time to move, that it was nothing personal but the building was being sold to a Wall Street man and his young wife. The Gambino brothers spoke the truth. Change is not personal but universal.

Now, I commute down to New York on a Metro North train from leafy Northern Westchester. The streets of New York are what I imagine the Ganges to be, a holy river. Walking there I see every state of human life pass: joy, sorrow, love, hate, wealth, homelessness, fame, misfortune. I remember that no state or feeling is final. Blocks away from The Limelight stood Barney's, a downtown department store that sold party clothes, maybe even to the woman I walked behind on the street the other day. And now it is the Rubin Museum of Art, offering sacred art and places for people to sit and be still in the midst of change.

"Love says 'I am everything.' Wisdom says 'I am nothing.' *Between the two, my life flows,"* taught the spiritual teacher Sri Nisargadatta Maharaj. *"My life flows"* is the key statement. Science and reason tell us we are limited, yet we don't feel limited. In the face of all the evidence to the contrary, we feel as if we are connected to everything. We overflow the banks of our own small lives and embrace the whole known world and all that is unknown beyond. How can this be?

This is how. There is a power in us that is not limited to us. I don't mean this in a misty, mystical sense. I mean "the force that through the green fuse drives the flower," to quote the poet Dylan Thomas. I mean the force that creates and pervades life, and destroys and creates. We remember this great power in the spring, when everything is bursting into bloom. There is often a tinge of sadness in spring, because in the midst of all that beauty, we can't help but remember other springs. In the plants and trees and the forward rushing life of the city, there is a reminder that we must, as the saying goes, let go or be dragged. We must find a way to be with life.

The Buddha described the state called *dukkha*, which is usually translated as "suffering" but which is closer to "unreliable" and "stressful." I once heard this pervasive state compared to the pain that comes from rubbing naked skin on a brick wall. It may not hurt much at first, but after a time it is a torment. This is the way things go, taught the Buddha. Nothing goes as smoothly as it does in our thoughts and dreams. Reality is rough, and we have a way of making it rougher. We brood about ourselves because nothing is exactly the way we want it to be, or stays fixed. Little rough patches begin to bleed.

Yet, we can find peace and equanimity. In places like the Rubin Museum and on our own (or even walking down the street in New York), we can learn to be with the endless ebb and flow of life. Mindfulness meditation is self-observation with compassion. It is the practice of returning home to the moment-by-moment sensory experience of being in a body, breathing in and out, open to all that arises. It is a simple practice, if not easy. It goes against the stream of life, and it is always an act of devotion.

> *The heart can think of no devotion*
> *Greater than being shore to the ocean.*
> *Holding the curve of one position,*
> *Counting an endless repetition.*
>
> —ROBERT FROST

On my way to Naropa, the engine in the van blew up, stranding us for days in western Illinois. Surrounded by cornfields, sweltering, desperate for distraction or something I couldn't name, I read books about the Gurdjieff Work. A distillation of the esoteric heart of the major spiritual traditions, expressed in a new language for the West by a brilliant Greek-Armenian spiritual master, the "Work" presented a way of being present in life, taking the obstacles and challenges that arise as a means to awaken. I thought I knew what it meant to be awake as opposed to asleep. But reading these books about ideas and ways of this mysterious, earthy, compelling Gurdjieff, it was if a bell rang deep inside me. For lack of a better word, I woke up to a new possibility, a new sense of what it meant to be present. The idea that there could be a way of being that unites the energies of body, heart, and mind—the possibility of a new level of being present—stirred to life.

That is why mindfulness. It's a beautiful lens and tool, easy to separate from its cultural trappings.

After decades of practice and retreats and friendship with leading Western teachers of mindfulness (*vipassana,* or insight, as it is often referred to in Asia), including Joseph Goldstein, Sharon Salzberg, Jack Kornfield, Gina Sharpe, and others, I trained as a "Community Dharma Leader" at the Spirit Rock Meditation Center. I went on many retreats. I teach at New York Insight and at the Rubin Museum. I lead my own *sangha* in Westchester.

As I practiced, I came to discover that there are moments that open up like doorways, that take me back to the extraordinary moment in the van—that moment when I thought all was lost.

And yet, I always thought life was the ultimate path. One of the most liberating and deeply formative experiences of my life was hearing the Gurdjieff idea about work in life.

TEACHING EXTERNAL AND INTERNAL

by Bart van Melik

A lot of people in New York are not aware of their ability to be aware externally. They are aware all the time. But it's not really in the forefront of their mind. It's not really concrete. It's never really framed as an external experience of, *"Oh I'm actually quite aware of my surroundings."* But you have to be.

When you take a bus and all of a sudden someone comes in and just looks at you a little too long, you know what to do. You look away, but you are still very aware of that person. Where is that person going to sit? What is that person going to do? Is that person sitting really close behind me on the bus? There's a heightened awareness. It's external.

So, a lot of times, I start teaching by talking about developing our awareness of the surroundings. Especially when students have possibly gone through trauma or they say, "I have a difficult time concentrating." Or maybe they say, "This awareness stuff is not for me." So, I'm starting from the external. And I tell them that same type of awareness can also be brought internally. Quite often in meditation you start by being aware of your body or your breath. But for people who are surrounded by so many things and so many people, it's sometimes better to start with their surroundings.

Also, start with the eyes open. Don't immediately start with the eyes closed. So, you are seeing. "Oh, I'm aware of my surroundings." What does that feel like? That's another important key when offering teaching of *dharma* to people who are in a very busy urban environment.

A lot of kids I teach don't have personal space. One group, who are in residential treatment, are in a cottage outside of the city. They're there because their parents or caretakers can't take care of them. Or sometimes because their own behavior is very challenging. Or they might be court-involved. I remember a fourteen-year-old boy in my class who used one teaching, one meditation, that I explore a lot. We call it "pause." And pause points to remember awareness. Remember that there might be more choices than your initial habitual response. So, we use it quite a lot as an instruction: "Oh, let's pause." "Let me pause." "Oh, let me be mindful again."

So, the boy came in after week ten of our series of classes and he said, *"Pause works."* I asked him why and he said:

> *I was in my room with my roommate and found out that he was using all kinds of stuff that belonged to me. And I immediately wanted to punch him in the face. My fist was clenched. Then I remembered the word "pause." Guess what, Bart? It didn't work. I still wanted to smack the shit out of him. But you know what I did? Because we've done it many times. It doesn't always work the first time. I paused again. Still wanted to punch him in the face. Then the third time I paused, I thought I'm going to get in trouble. I do not want to stay here longer. And I just decided to move away. And when I was calm, I said, "Don't take my stuff."*

These are little tiny anecdotes—but they're big—about how this practice works.

I also remember a girl who was in the detention center. When you're in the detention center, quite often you have to go to court, and nothing happens and then you have to go back. She said:

I went to court the other day, Bart. And I was so nervous. The practice didn't help calm me down at all. I tried. I did mindful breathing. It didn't work at all. I still was so, so nervous. I still was really aware that my future was on the line. I might do a lot of years upstate. To be honest, the whole experience was terrifying to me. But, when I came back in the hall with the other girls, we always ask, how was it? All of a sudden I realized I remembered everything the judge said. The previous times I would go into the courtroom and I would still feel awful the same way. Meditation didn't help that much. But I would forget everything. I didn't even hear what they were saying. So, it works in a different way for me. I can still be open to information in the midst of feeling totally afraid and fearful. So, it kind of works. My mind was easeful.

That's another element of the practice. You can still be in the midst of a lot of *dukkha* and still be open to what is going on—both internally and externally.

Lots of the neighborhoods that these kids that I teach come from are neighborhoods where there are lots of challenges. If you really look at New York City, it is pretty segregated. For example, the majority of the kids whom I teach are coming from the Bronx, which is the poorest county in the United States and it sits next to the richest, Manhattan.

You might think that growing up in New York City as an adolescent, they would know the city. But I've asked a lot of my Bronx students if they've ever been to Union Square and they ask, "What's Union Square?"

So that's one element. A lot of the kids stay in the neighborhood they were born in and they live in, and they suffer from the intensity of all these people living together. Some of the middle schools hold way too many kids. Some of the kids I taught are from immigrant families and they told me they would love to practice meditation but they are sharing a two-bedroom apartment with two other families. There is hardly any personal space. And that translates as having no mental space, too; not having enough space to concentrate for homework or to come back to oneself for a moment.

For me, as a teacher, I can be aware externally where the students are and maybe incorporate what they already bring in. So now the fidget spinner is a big thing. One group of kids in residential treatment come to practice meditation twice a week. They all bring their spinners. We include them in the meditation—have them all spin and just be aware of their thumb going around, their eyes seeing.

But, sometimes the teaching is not what I expect. Instead of the spinner, what about a phone? Once I was leading a meditation in a school and I asked the girls to put their phones away. One girl got upset with me constantly asking her to put her phone away. Then she just put it in her shirt and said, *"Come and get it."*

I decided in that moment, luckily because I was feeling grounded, *I'm going to meditate out loud.* While the entire class of twenty-six was looking at me, I told them,

> *"I'm just going to say out loud what's happening in me. My heart is pounding. I'm aware of feeling tension. And now that I'm actually having everyone's attention, including yours,"* I told the girl, *"I feel a sense of being seen. And that leads to a sense of more calmness. And now I'm also starting to feel my breath again, which I totally lost. And I'm feeling a fact that I can be open to what you've done and I feel okay to share*

with you that it landed for me as a feeling. I felt disrespected. That's all. Thank you."

And I continued the meditation and she didn't use the phone. It just stayed where it was. At the end of the class, she came up to me and she said, "That was all right."

And that only happened, I think, because there was some room in my mind to be still creative in the midst of my buttons being so pushed. So I certainly believe that I've made a lot of personal development simply because of having to show up for all of these communities. Practicing for myself while I'm teaching or sharing the *dharma*.

I think it's a great responsibility and at the same time a privilege to be of service in this way. It's something that doesn't feel like a chore to me to do it. But there was a time when I was offering on a weekly basis to seventeen communities of practice and I would do retreats annually. And all of them were of a very different nature.

At the moment, I've cut back on weekly classes. So, I'm going to about ten weekly communities in New York, some retreats in places in the United States and Europe, and some monthly classes. The fact that I get to teach so much to so many different communities helps me to stay on the path. I would not have been so diligent in my own practice if I hadn't had the support of all of these communities who would show up. And if I'm not practicing and I show up, it really reflects in my teaching. And I would hear back. They would tell me, "Bart, you're talking too much in your instructions. What's wrong with you?" That honesty. And I have to be real and say, "Oh, you're right."

Also, really practicing self-knowledge. Because I think that's what awareness does. It gives you information about what you're doing. And your habits.

And this has changed my practice.

When I started practice, I had a strong emphasis on the technique of practicing meditation and there was a hidden agenda of trying to attain specific concentration states that I thought were necessary for relief of stress and to see more clearly. And I still see the value of that. But I'm not clinging so much to a specific technique, or thinking I need to attain a specific state to make progress on this path. And I really started to see that it's much more about this radical willingness to be present with what is.

In my offering of meditation to young people or people who have had a lot of trauma, I was kind of forced to be as simple and concrete as possible. And that I've taken into my own practice as well.

It's also about language. A very important element about bringing the *dharma* into the world is being aware of what type of language we use. And sometimes it's helpful to bring in the Buddha's teaching very specifically in naming the Buddha because people who have a faith-oriented vibe, they will really take to it. Wow. There's someone who really let go of greed, hatred, and delusion. It's possible. A human being did that.

But it's not always helpful to bring that in. In schools or juvenile detention centers, especially with youth, I'll sometimes say "a wise teacher." I sometimes will use the word "Buddha." But I was working in a homeless shelter and one of my students, Mohammad, fourteen years old, was really taking to the practice. All of a sudden, he wasn't there anymore. And I talked to the staff and they said, well, Mohammad's mom found out you guys were doing meditation and they're Muslim and so they thought that was not good for Mohammad to be there. So I asked the staff if they could invite the mom for the following week and she came with another mom. I so appreciated that they were open to come to the class. And they ended up doing the class.

I think it's so important to bring in the body. So, we do a lot of movement with young folks. And both of the moms were doing all kinds of stretches and they did the meditation. And at the end of class, she just said, "Oh, that's fine. Mohammad can come next week. I just had to check."

So, it really depends on the context. The veterans who are adults also ask me questions about where does this stuff come from. And then I will go into the Buddha's teaching.

It's like this: If you just come and say we're going to meditate right now and they have to sit still, first of all, what does that mean? And some of them already put their thumb against their index finger and go, "OMMM. I saw this on TV. Bart, am I meditating?"

It makes more sense to start with a contemplation and talk about a universal aspect of being human. For example, fear. Maybe I will ask everyone, "What are your top two fears?" And then we all hear from one another. One says, "I start to think, Oh, I'm not the only one with fear." There are always a few guys who say "I'm fearless," but then as they hear someone say, "Roaches in the bathtub," they go, "Oh. Me, too. I'm afraid of roaches."

When you're doing this together, you start to see that you have your own stuff. But when you really start to hear it from other people, too, then you're sharing this experience of suffering. You're sharing this experience of what it's like to not hold on to stuff for a moment and your mind is easeful. It's so important to create community for young folks and for all the groups that we can offer practice to. And it's important that people hear from one another.

Sometimes my class ends up being not what I planned at all. And if I cling to my plan, I'm suffering, but if I'm just meeting them where they are, we might end up having a long conversation about inspirational figures in our lives. And we all walk away highly inspired. We didn't do any stretching, we didn't do any meditating, but we formed a group.

What I call the kids who are in difficult situations, challenging situations, who are often called youth at risk or vulnerable youth within the policy world, is resilient. I actually see the resilience, the resiliency within them.

I go to a juvenile detention center in the Bronx and I teach groups both of girls and of boys. There were five in the group of girls, and three really wanted to do the practice. In our discussion, before we would go into practice, we talked about our hero or shero, and one girl talked about her mom a lot. She also talked about a girlfriend of hers from the neighborhood, the same age, whom she really misses and who is also court-involved. And every time when she needs support, she thinks about her girlfriend.

The following week she's so happy. She comes to me and says, "Remember I talked about this girlfriend of mine? Ta da. Here she is in prison with me." And we sit together, this time the four of us. And we talk about inspiration. The girl who talked about her mom and her friend who is now also in jail says that she really feels like her friend has her back because she's here right now. I say, "I really appreciate that you guys found each other. But wasn't it by chance that you came here and now sit together?" The new girl said, "No. I actually had the chance to be either in a nonsecure facility or a secure facility. And I found out my friend was in a secure, locked facility, so I asked if they could place me in here just to be with her."

She's telling me like she's telling me I had oatmeal this morning. "We're friends. We have each other's back. She would have done the same thing for me."

It's really hard being in that particular facility. That is where kids are waiting for their sentences, and then they might have to do more time or they have to do an alternative program. Here we are. She chose to be in an environment she knew was not easy. There is a lot of external stress happening. Staff is overworked. Kids sometimes end up in fights. And she chose to be there just to be with her friend.

That's just one example of the enormous power and deep value of friendship that is there. And the importance of showing up.

It's also really important, especially for kids who have gone through a lot, and also for veterans who have gone through a lot of institutions, that the teacher always shows up. The other week, I had to do an evaluation at the juvenile detention center and so they had to fill out a questionnaire. And one question was, "What do you like about the meditation program?" One girl just said, "Bart." And I asked, "Why?" She said, "You're always there. Just the fact that you show up and we can come together as a group." That is key.

The one thing that really drew me to this practice is its self-empowering quality. The Buddha talked about "come and see for yourself."

Growing up in Holland in a secular society, not growing up with a lot of institutional religion myself, there was an emphasis on science: let science prove things that are hard to explain.

And when I came to Buddhism, I liked the fact that I didn't have to assume anything. And I liked the fact that it is about cultivating qualities of mind that support kindness, both within myself and in the society.

The reason I go to places where people are who have gone through a lot is that I'm not so much there to offer another thing that they need in terms of self-help. But much more something that they can come check for themselves to see if that could be something that could work.

One thing that I really appreciate about bringing the Buddha's teachings—even though I'll pack it often in a secular way—is that they have that empowering quality of come and see for yourself. Is this something that you can use for yourself to ease your mind and to release anger? To release a sense of stress? And after doing it for about nine years, I see it works. So, at first I had this faith that I could maybe offer something. And that slowly transferred, from what I heard as feedback, that people really took on this practice as something that they could do for themselves. And they could eventually do in community.

TRAINING UNDERGROUND

by Joshua Bee Alafia (Jbee)

Like most of the inspirations that move me in life and have lasting impact on my journey, this one starts with a dream. I was nineteen and had had a few experiences sitting with Tibetan meditation teachers in Santa Cruz, California, while at college. I was home for the summer and dreamed of walking into a subway car that was completely filled with Tibetan monks in robes, chanting. I sat and joined them, chanting along in unison, and had the realization that subway cars are actually moving temples. The power of the experience raised my heart rate and woke me up.

That realization sparked the practice of training underground—a regular practice for me these last seventeen years living in New York City—concentrating on passengers, closing my eyes, and picturing them thriving and joyful, often in a state of bliss. Later, I would learn that this practice is a version of giving *metta,* unconditional love and lovingkindness practice.

> *In this way, in regard to the body one abides contemplating the body internally . . . externally . . . both internally and externally. One abides contemplating the nature of arising . . . of passing away . . . of both arising and passing away in the body. Mindfulness that 'there is a body' is established in one to the extent necessary for bare knowledge and continuous mindfulness. And one abides independent, not clinging to*

anything in the world. That too is how in regard to the body one abides contemplating the body.

—GAUTAMA BUDDHA, *SATIPATTHANA SUTTA*

Descending the stairs into the burrow of the A train, I feel a damp breeze, the bass of wind and steel on steel resonates in my chest. I pick up my pace in case my train is pulling in; turn the corner to see the sound is coming from the other side of the platform. I can slide my Metro Card and go through the turnstile leisurely. The downtown train on the other side carries subterranean tailwinds as it pulls off and the roar softens into the distance.

I find my waiting place beside the tracks and look down the dark tunnel for any signs of an oncoming train, then smile to myself, realizing the breeze always precludes the train's headlights. Three dark grey rats scamper playfully about the tracks. One, surveying a semi-crushed soda cup from the pizza place upstairs and seemingly disappointed by the contents, rushes off to catch up with its friends.

I settle into my body; my knees bend slightly. The bending of the knees in standing meditation always makes me smile, as that is the instruction given to keep one from falling asleep standing up. I feel alert as I contemplate sensations in the body internally and externally. I can still feel the pressure on my ankle from where my son sat on my lap as I read to him, minutes prior to me running to catch this train. I feel the moisture of sweat on my forehead from the subway dash. I smell the blend of urine, cologne, laundry detergent, pizza, and Jamaican curry (not necessarily in that order) that perfumes the corner of Nostrand and Fulton avenues. I can hear someone playing Sade's *"Your Love is King"* through the vents that connect the subway to the sidewalk. I notice how my awareness

around me.
ere they are
projecting
even go as
ferred. The
be happy!" I

ng-out of sensations, sounds, smells, the
going.

lly, my personal abracadabra of mindful-
awareness of sensation, of being in the
el the weight of the body in my high-tops.
nal level of the planet earth. *"I am rooted."*
lling as I breathe. My breaths begin to
tions of rushing leaves me.

can't believe I've never seen her live. She's
he's so beautiful. I wonder what she's like.
Could we possibly fall in love? But she's
n to move to Brooklyn? . . . Whoa. There is

ning me. My abdomen rises. My abdo-
handles kissing up against my beltline.
always have that li'l extra love handle. I
of this body. There is a body." I feel the
eeling the expanse. My spine cracks as
my lower back. Breathing in. Feeling
ath.

ead. Breathing in the breeze, I see the
coming. I feel my weight in my feet. *"I*
rain races toward my body. I bring all
lightness in my left foot. The train
doors past me. I lift my left leg and
eeling awareness in my feet and notic-
ttle corner, standing right against the
es have mostly neutral expressions. I

see what looks like sadness in the eyes of some of the people
Perhaps it's just a mild disdain of the process of getting to wh
going. Perhaps their faces are just relaxed in thought and I'r
my own conditioned perceptions of what sadness looks like.
far as perceiving their expressions as the look of dreams d
mind, the ultimate storyteller, the griot of griots! "*May you*
extend to my fellow passengers.

TRAFFIC AS A VEHICLE FOR AWAKENING

by Diana Gould

Living in Los Angeles is a little like living in a castle surrounded by a moat in which lives a fire-breathing dragon. In order to leave the house and go anywhere, you have to first do battle with this beast—a struggle so draining that one hesitates before embarking upon it, often opting to stay home rather than enter the fray. And yet, inevitably one has to leave the house; to go to work, go to events, go to places of interest, go out to see other people, and so, one must develop strategies for getting past the dragon. The dragon in the analogy is traffic.

It is virtually impossible for any two Angelinos to have a conversation without mentioning traffic. It is the inescapable ordeal we all live with. During peak traffic times—meaning, the times when you and everybody else needs to go somewhere—the time it takes to get anywhere has more than doubled. What used to take twenty minutes now can take over an hour. It's hard to get it through your head how much time you have to allow to get anywhere. A study done three years ago found that people in Los Angeles spent an average of ninety-two hours a year stuck in traffic. That seems low to me; it must be more by now. But that means, if you work an eight-hour day, five days a week, with two weeks off for vacation, you spend more time stuck in traffic than you get for your vacation. It is the first noble truth of living in Los Angeles. There is suffering, and there is traffic.

Since it cannot be avoided, can it be transcended? Is there a spiritual solution to being stuck in traffic?

Yes, and perhaps the word "stuck" is the key.

When difficult emotions overtake us, we feel we are in their grip—"stuck." Either we're caught on a hamster wheel of repeating and rehashing the incident we're regretting or resenting, or we are unable to budge from our fixed position, holding a point of view or opinion very much at odds with one or more opponents. Perhaps we can use our difficulties in traffic to stand as a metaphor for the obstacles we face in the rest of our life. Perhaps traffic is the perfect vehicle for awakening. Perhaps we can even reach a stage where we are grateful for traffic jams because of the opportunity they provide to learn and practice techniques that will serve us in other areas of our lives.

Or not. But at least we can learn how to have a healthier response to being caught in traffic.

If traffic is the first noble truth, then the second noble truth is its cause. While the scientific cause of traffic might be more cars entering the road than the road can handle, requiring cars to slow down to let them, which then causes a wave of slowing reaching back for miles; the cause of suffering in traffic is wanting it to be different. The speed limit is sixty-five mph, you are going between two and five mph. You don't want it to be that way, but it is. Our first response is usually to get angry, either at ourselves for not leaving sooner, or at the other cars and drivers for preventing us from getting where we need to be. But where does that get you? You can stew in frustration, anger, resentment, exasperation—or you can let go.

Letting go is the third noble truth. It is a general, all-purpose solution to almost any problem we face. Let go of the way you wish it could be, the way you would prefer it to be, and the way that it would be if only you ran the world (to the world's great benefit), and respond skillfully to the way that it is.

A skillful response to being stuck in traffic begins with practicing mindfulness. Begin with body sensations. Notice the tension in the muscles, in the shoulders, in the hands gripping the wheel. Sometimes all that's necessary is to open to the truth of the way it is—tension, tightness, gripping, clenched jaw, gritted teeth—to open up a bit of space, or spaciousness, for the gripping and tightness to ease. Telling tension not to be there is as futile as telling the other cars to get off the road. But by noticing the body sensations, allowing them to be there, investigating them without resistance, we can create the space for them to fluctuate. And when we can tune in to their fluctuations, we create the space for them to dissolve.

A curious function of impermanence: what you resist, persists. If you resist the tension, it freezes it in the body, causing stress and blockage in the muscles and arteries, increasing blood pressure, and causing tightness, stiffness, and spasm in the muscles. When you allow the tension to be there, open to it, accept and investigate it, noticing the tiny variations, the pulsations and vibrations, you open the space for it to dissolve into impermanence and flow.

Similarly, being stuck in traffic offers many opportunities to observe unwholesome mind states arising. Anger at ourselves for not allowing enough time, or at the other drivers for cutting in front of us, for changing lanes, or simply for existing; fear of being late; shame and guilt, as we project our condemnation onto the waiting party; dishonesty, as we rehearse the lie we will give as an excuse, blaming traffic when in truth, had we left in time, traffic could have been accommodated. Aggression, competitiveness, ego, frustration—traffic gives us endless opportunities to watch the arising of unwholesome mind states.

When we practice unwholesome mind states without mindfulness, they result in stress, difficulty, and unhappiness to ourselves and others. Yet the Buddha tells us that all we need do when unwholesome mind states arise—as they inevitably will—is notice their arising, and rather than nurture or feed them, abandon them. We have no control over the thoughts that arise in our mind. But we do have control over our response to them. We can feed, nurture, repeat, and "retweet" them, or we can recognize them as unwholesome, and let them go. We can use them as an opportunity to learn about the nature of self, of ego, with its tendency to prioritize our wishes over those of others, and we can use "right effort" to choose a more wholesome response, such as kindness, generosity, patience, and equanimity.

Patience, according to the Buddha, is "the supreme virtue." It is one of the *paramis*, the qualities necessary for liberation and enlightenment. Patience is the ability to be with the difficult and the unpleasant in a non-reactive way.

From the moment we are born, when we are yanked out of a womb where we were housed and fed effortlessly as we floated with ease in amniotic fluid, only to be spanked, then gazed at lovingly as we're held in our mother's arms, only to become tired, hungry, or wet, life is a series of ups and downs. Much as we might like a life where we encounter only pleasant sensations and gratifying experiences, this is not the case for any of us, no matter how fortunate. This is the first noble truth of suffering, as the Buddha has taught, and it is true for everyone. Life includes many moments that are difficult, unpleasant, irritating, aggravating, infuriating—a whole spectrum of circumstances, which have as their common root that we don't like them. And they are inevitable. Patience is the quality that allows us to respond to unpleasant circumstances with courage, perseverance, acceptance, forbearance, and forgiveness.

Patience is the opposite of compulsive behavior and reactivity. It requires effort and intention. Patience means not succumbing to anger, aggression, or despair when threatened. It means being mindful of our reactions and emotional responses. There is no more excellent training in this virtue than being stuck in traffic.

When we are unable to get where we want to go in the time we want it to take, due to traffic congestion resulting from accident, construction, or simply too many other people wanting to go someplace at the same time, we can get angry and upset, but what good does it do? Does it get us there faster? Does it result in any benefit to ourselves or anyone else? Alternatively, if we practice patience, we are learning a skill that will be valuable in many other circumstances.

Patience has many levels. The most basic is grit-your-teeth-and-get-through-it endurance. The next level is forbearance, using self-control and tolerance, allowing the situation to be as it is. Ultimately, patience can be a form of forgiveness, liberating ourselves from any feeling of anger or resentment, recognizing the truth of the way it is, and letting go of any expectation that it be different.

Generosity is another of these *paramis*, or wholesome qualities. In the West, we tend to associate Buddhism with meditation. In the time of the Buddha, however, the gradual training began not with meditation, but with generosity, because it is a training in letting go. Generosity is the opposite of clinging, holding on, and craving (causes of suffering); it is the act of releasing, opening, and allowing, a recognition of the equality and interdependence of all (effecting the end of suffering). Generosity is related to karma, the law of cause and effect. When the Buddha was asked to describe karma, he said, *"There is what is given."* Or, as the Beatles put it, *"The love you take is equal to the love you make."*

I like to think of generosity as conceding the space between the way it is and the way I'd like it to be. Treating each driver the way I'd like to be treated myself—with kindness, caring, and compassion. Allowing other cars to enter our lane. Letting others go first. Not honking our horn in rebuke. Giving other drivers the benefit of the doubt. Understanding that nobody's perfect, least of all us.

The four *Brahmaviharas,* translated as "dwelling places of the gods," are four qualities that are innate in every one of us, but need to be practiced, developed, and—to the best of our ability—perfected. They are the most wholesome mind states, and minds that are imbued with these qualities experience the ultimate happiness. The words in English are awkward in translation, but they are lovingkindness or friendliness (*metta*), sympathetic or empathetic joy (*mudita*), compassion (*karuna*), and equanimity (*upekkha*). Practicing these qualities on the streets and freeways of Los Angeles is the fast way to Buddhahood, even if it is the slow way to get anywhere else.

We can practice *metta,* or lovingkindness, by sending thoughts of well-wishing to other drivers sharing the road with us. One way we learn to do this in meditation is by repeating phrases, such as, *"May you be happy and peaceful," "May you be safe and protected,"* using each phrase as an intention, not pretending to feel something we do not, but a recognition of the value of the benefit of this kindness. There is no downside to wishing for the happiness and safety of the other drivers on the road with you, and it is a lot more beneficial for our own nervous system and well-being than wishing they'd go to hell.

Meditators cultivate these qualities by repeating the phrases, in meditation, towards various categories of beings, beginning with ourselves, eventually including loved ones, mentors, friends, "neutral" people who we know slightly but have no feelings towards, enemies, and eventually all beings without exception. One phrase I like to use is, *"May I awaken to my radiant true nature as boundless love."* As I am someone who usually has a song going round and round in my head, I give each *metta* phrase a little tune. Once, on retreat, I spent a lot of time visualizing the streets and roads on which I'm often stuck in traffic, picturing the people in all the cars smiling to each other and singing, *"May we awaken to our radiant true nature as boundless love."* Now, when I find myself trapped on these same streets and roads, the image returns, and it makes me laugh and feel more kindly toward the people in the other cars.

Mudita is taking pleasure in the happiness of others. Rejoicing in the good fortune of the one who made the left turn before the light changed, even if you are still stuck now that it's red, might take a lot of practice, but as the Dalai Lama has pointed out, if you take happiness from the happiness of others, and there are six billion others, you increase the odds of your own happiness six billion to one.

Compassion, *karuna*, is the third of these *Brahmaviharas*. How often has it happened that you are frustrated at the pace at which traffic is moving, only to drive past its cause: a catastrophic accident in which people were undoubtedly seriously injured or worse? Frustration can quickly turn to compassion. Perhaps we can practice compassion even without needing such a drastic motivating factor. For surely, just as you are experiencing frustration, so is everyone else in this traffic jam. Compassion is an ability to feel tenderness towards the suffering of another, and to hold their suffering without turning from it. It is a recognition of our common humanity.

Equanimity, *upekkha,* the last of these qualities, is the recognition of impermanence. It is the opposite of attachment. Equanimity is the awareness that all things change, and the ability to be with the difficult without rejecting it, the pleasant without clinging to it. Equanimity is the understanding that even this traffic jam, which seems so intractable and unyielding, will, in fact and in time, change.

The Buddha tells us that there is no thing that exists separate from the conditions that gave rise to it. This is helpful to remember when stuck in traffic. There is not "me" over here, and "traffic" over there; we are, as Einstein pointed out, part of an indivisible whole called the universe. Although we experience ourselves as something separate from the rest, this is in fact a kind of optical delusion of consciousness.

In other words, I am not stuck in traffic: I *am* traffic.

Perhaps the best method of dealing with the difficulties of driving in Los Angeles is the one that, in this city at this time, might be the most challenging, the most arduous, the least convenient, but in the end, the most beneficial for the most sentient beings, now and in the future: use public transportation.

STILL, IN THE PEDALS

by Paul Irving

The entrance to your path is anywhere you turn,
and each step along it as natural as breathing.
Follow this path and soon it will seem
as familiar as the garden walkway
behind your home,
for you will have found your path
in the original dream
where all paths lead inevitably to the Whole.

It is like a cut-glass bowl on a moonlit night
when we can no longer tell the sparkling container
from the glittering water it contains.
Do you see? There is nothing to get excited about.
We are talking about an ordinary glass bowl.
Just a bowl. And water, just water.

—MORTON MARCUS,

FROM *THE EIGHT ECSTASIES OF YAEKO IWASAKI*

Early each morning I throw my leg over the bike seat and head down Dolores Street in San Francisco's Mission neighborhood with a clear and firm intention to bring the practice of meditation from the cushion into the street. With the sweet thrill of increasing speed and the sting of the cold morning air on my cheeks and ears, I murmur a quiet wish for safety, a prayer for myself and for all bike commuters. Perhaps this little ritual is the remnant of each family outing begun with a prayer (a quick Hail Mary for short trips, a full rosary for long ones) or maybe just the awareness that at any time causes and conditions much larger than myself could take me on a ride I would rather not take.

Those mornings when I'm on point, when the anxiety *du jour* has fallen away, the magic of simply being present opens before me and an unlikely stillness pervades my body. How can this be, how can I fly down a steep hill on two wheels, navigating stop lights and road hazards, negotiating the in-between spaces of cars and curbs, and yet feel as still as a granite wall in the high Sierras?

Even at this early hour, homeless folks who live in the neighborhood begin emerging from the doorways and bushes that have afforded some protection throughout the night. I murmur more wishes, prayers for their safety, prayers that today they find comfort.

Crossing Market Street, I tuck into a narrow, one-block bike path, closed to cars at both ends and set between the exterior wall of a cavernous twenty-four-hour grocery and the steep face of a rock promontory that is home to the US Mint in San Francisco. The block-long canyon formed by these two icons of capitalism is a favorite place for junkies to shoot up, to find short-lived comfort from their daily suffering. (On Tuesday nights, a short Buddhist monk in crimson robes and tennis shoes who always seems to be laughing offers warmth and clean needles to all comers.) The early morning light, gold-yellow reflected off the grocery wall mural, again brings me back to a solid stillness, an internal quiet that, although often not apparent, is somehow always available.

In the ancient Buddhist writings, "going into homelessness" is the term used to describe giving oneself completely to the life and teachings of the Buddha, leaving one's family and livelihood and choosing the beggar's bowl and the company of fellow itinerants as a way of life. It is a beautiful path of singular focus. Although I have great respect and profound admiration for those who have followed that path, I have chosen to live within and hold intimately the many contradictions of urban life.

These are the challenges of the householder, of those practicing in the hum and whir of city life: to stay immersed in the tensions of the world, negotiating the in-between spaces; to bring stillness to all action; to justly acquire and use one's resources for the benefit of one's self, one's family, and one's community; to drink deeply from the sorrows and the joys of the world; and to demonstrate kindness, wisdom, and compassion to the best of one's ability in each moment.

It started in the 1970s when I was just a young teen. Dad and I watched Merv Griffin interview a famous meditation guru. Something indescribable clicked. The conversation awakened a profound longing, the possibility of stillness, that even as a youngster seemed so familiar, yet a destination that was much too far to reach on my own. In hindsight, some forty years later, the reasons for that longing are less obscure now than they were then. Being one of five children might have more than a little to do with longing for quiet. As my gay sexuality was just beginning to emerge, perhaps I was longing for safety, for sanctuary from the harsh judgment of white, middle class, heterosexual Catholicism, for protection from my own condemnation as well. Yes, to all of those reasons, and likely many more that are yet to become apparent. And yes, to the profound, ineffable desire to return to the inward stillness that is our home and our birthright.

Known for his candor and insightful wit, Suzuki Roshi, the now-famous monk who founded the San Francisco Zen Center, apocryphally addressed a room of Zen students: "When I look out at you, all I see is enlightened beings . . . until you open your mouths." What was it he was seeing? What is it in me that was here before my parents were born, that links me to all bike commuters, to the homeless seeking comfort, to workers at the grocery and the Mint, to the short monk in tennis shoes? What is it that connects me across time to all living beings?

Lately I'm not so keen on calm. For the first half of these forty years of practice, I quietly nurtured an internal barometer, a timeworn score card measuring each meditation period against the last. Frequently "calm" was in no way evident; more often than not the daily "calm" tally dipped below zero. And then, every so often, I would be enveloped in a deep quiet, mysteriously finding myself in a place of profound reverence for every detail of my life. It was those moments I longed for. If only I could figure it out, learn to navigate that path directly, keep the experience going just a bit longer.

Then, the unspoken goal, the motivation to interrupt the flow of the workaday world and sit quietly without stimulation, was to calm myself, to achieve an inner state of stillness. Largely it didn't work. At increasingly subtle levels it became just another achievement to attain, another Oz that was perpetually beyond my reach. It was so close, yet I could never quite grasp it. Clearly, I was doing something wrong. I told myself I just needed to meditate longer, to sharpen my focus, to double down on the effort. If only I knew a deeper, truer, more profound truth, then I would have the stillness I longed for.

In the mid-1990s, suffering from a spinal cord injury, my search for inner stillness took a turn. At a mindfulness class offered by a local hospital, I learned to simply watch my mind, to stop trying to make it calm.

Toward the end of the two-month class series, a full-day retreat was offered, a day to simply be in silence. I vividly recall arriving at the unfamiliar conference center, nervous at the thought of a whole day without speaking, nervous yet excited at the prospect of utter quiet. That lovely aspiration lasted for about half an hour.

Boom . . . boom . . . boom . . . an enormous bass drum thundered— and from very close by—each beat resonating in my chest. Soon the syncopated rhythms from many drums joined in. *"What? Is this a drum convention?"* Quite apparently, the center's master scheduler failed to recognize an inherent conflict between a meditation group and a Taiko drum ensemble. And so it went for nearly eight hours.

For the first few of those hours the drums were more annoying, more irritating than all the noise and activity of the city combined. But then something shifted. Just at the point when I felt tied up in knots, I finally understood what our valiant teachers were telling us: this is how it is just now, invite it in, stop resisting it, notice your reactions, see if there is the possibility of simply being present to just as it is right now, including your annoyance and frustration and all your ideas and beliefs about how this is not the way it is supposed to be. Nothing to push away nor hold onto, just observing the stream of moment-to-moment experience. When I stopped trying to push away the pulsing beat, my mind and heart immediately relaxed and began to settle into a profound inner quiet, a quiet that was in no way in conflict with the intricate Taiko rhythms. No longer the center of my focus, the sound of the drums became just part of the aural landscape, much the way a quiet songbird or babbling brook does on a warm summer day in the country, neither demanding nor escaping attention.

After that experience, the practice of meditation became really interesting. I was simply being with the noise in my own head, the noise of my family, the neighbors, and the whole city; letting go of my internal demand that this moment be any different than it is.

Twenty years on, and now a meditation teacher myself, I imagine those teachers in wide-eyed panic as the drumming began. *"Wait, wait, they can't do that. We have a whole class of beginning meditators. They're not ready for this level of challenge."* Despite our best efforts to make a quiet clearing, to find a refuge of silence, life breaks in: morning crows making a racket, the neighbors arguing again, the construction crew across the street starting early this month. And those are only minor distractions compared to the cacophonous symphony between my own ears.

Despite any panic those teachers may have felt, they continued to encourage us to loosen our grip on the demand that meditation should look like calm serenity, guiding us to just be present with our moment-to-moment experience, to watch our minds fight against, bargain with, and try to manipulate the pounding drumbeat, and to do so without judgment or recrimination of the drummers, the situation, or ourselves.

By day's end, it was apparent that although the master scheduler may not have intended it, programming the two groups together was in no way a failure. The drumming had been a gift. In the face of the overwhelming torrent of sound it was futile to continue demanding silence, insisting that the situation be any different than it was.

In the letting go, the paradox became apparent: only through being with, staying present to the commotion and noise around us does stillness become possible. Stillness and silence are less concerned with the absence of activity and sound than with abandoning our efforts to resist the reality of the present moment. Said differently, the experience of stillness is not dependent on the external circumstances of our lives, the noise or silence in our neighborhoods, homes, or even within our own heads; rather, it is the experience of dropping into the unconditioned stillness in which we already dwell. Perhaps this is what Suzuki Roshi was pointing toward: there is no future state to achieve. The possibility of awakening is always present, yet mostly we are too enchanted with our own opinions and voices to notice.

Continuing my morning journey, I wiggle through the lower Haight and climb the Page Street hill heading toward the infamous Haight-Ashbury neighborhood. Pedaling through these quiet streets of million-dollar gentrified homes, the once working-class neighborhood that loudly proclaimed Free Love seems like a long-forgotten dream. On my way to a well-paying job and with the memory of the US Mint atop its promontory still vivid in my mind, I wonder what happened to that longing for love, free or otherwise. Have we sold out or simply bought in?

On warm evenings and weekends, these streets are juxtaposed with affluent shoppers searching for the dream (if not of free love, at least of deep discounts) and homeless twenty-somethings in sandals and dirty tie-dyed tees hoping for spare change. For me, these shoppers and vagabonds are emblematic of one of the greatest tensions of urban living: those with the fortune of relative financial security enjoy the comfort and protection of steady housing, while those without such fortune search for comfort and protection wherever they can find it, beneath a bush or in a doorway, or more recently, in nylon ripstop tents lined edge-to-edge along the few remaining industrial areas of the city.

Rolling through these neighborhoods, still and still moving, I hold these contradictions with the heartache of compassion. In that stillness is the profound conviction that shopper and vagabond and cyclist are all of one piece, connected in the most elemental manner. But for the causes and conditions of my life, of their lives, these shoppers and transient urban dwellers are not separate from me, I am not apart from them. The murmured wishes for my own safety and comfort are prayers for their safety and comfort as well.

PAVEMENT PRACTICE

by Angela Dews

I have arrived. I am home. On Malcolm X Boulevard in Harlem, New York. Having the intention to lift, then swing, then place my foot, looking down with softened gaze to see where I'm stepping. A safe place to land. No dog poop. The uneven sidewalk can be negotiated. No holes or sharp things.

I look up and check the line of *sangha* members walking in front of me. Walking meditation is not as slow on the Boulevard as it is when we're inside the yoga studio, but also not so fast that we blend in with the Sunday afternoon shoppers, just coming from church, on their way to brunch.

Very respectful they are. They wait for us to pass. Then, since I'm last, I see them hurry on to one of the places where they might sit down and order or where they might choose from the hot buffet of greens or callaloo, ribs or ham, mac and cheese and banana pudding.

I hand out cards explaining who we are, and where and when they can come and join the Harlem Sit by donation; all are welcome; no experience is necessary; based on the teachings of the Buddha but not requiring changing beliefs or adopting new belief systems.

So far, only one person said she saw us on the street and that is why she came. But we've changed locations and moved to two different yoga studios and then to the rectory house tucked behind a church built in 1890 where we walk in the yard across from the police precinct. And send the merit of our practice to ripple out to all beings without exception.

But, when we were in our storefront on the street, we had the experience of the street. I would occasionally slip outside and ask someone to turn down the car radio for the next fifteen minutes, while we finished our meditation. "Sure," they always said.

And, we experienced the feelings of sympathetic joy, *mudita*, when the church next door released the children at the end of Sunday School. The Dalai Lama has said that *mudita* for the joy of all the others in the world gives us six billion chances to feel happiness. My instruction to the *sangha* was to feel the annoyance as the sounds landed on our space, on our ears, and also see if we could feel the way the joy felt externally and then internally, sharing the freedom feelings of the children as they felt the need to holler and stamp their feet because they were outside of church, outside our window.

Pavement practice in New York is many things.

We meet image after image created and displayed for us to desire. And the beings aren't in cars and they don't actually invite us to cross over the blurred lines between public and private. But they are moving and morphing and showing off. So, we can spectate and overhear and have opinions—that's lovely and I want it; and that's goofy and I don't get it; and that should not even be allowed on the sidewalk.

And I love it here, where I'm not the craziest person or the ugliest person or the prettiest. Of course, I probably never was. But the city offers a particular safety in that regard.

On a good day, noticing when I'm off balance. And maybe noticing the flavor of how the sights land, the sounds land, and how my foot lands, and catching myself before I make up a story and react—based on habits and the notion of who I am, who I have always been.

Once, when I was newly sober and clean, I was walking down Ninth Avenue past a liquor store and saw a big bottle of gin on sale. It stopped me in my tracks. I knew I was going to drink again eventually at some point and the price was amazing. I skipped over it then, but in that moment was the direct experience of rationalizing, ignoring, and justifying away all the things I knew about my habit patterns. Feeling the familiarity of wanting.

Instead, I paused. And before I went in, I called a friend from a phone booth (they were on the sidewalk in front of stores in those days). I didn't mean *not* to buy the gin, but to put it off. So far, I have still put it off.

People are drinking outside everywhere these days, but in New York, I get to see the rich and famous and gorgeous sipping their cocktails, laughing, being fabulous, having fun at sidewalk cafe tables sitting in my way as I go about my business.

I remember what I had to tell myself when I was just starting to stop, and the drinking looked so appealing, and the drinkers looked so cool: I won't look like that after a few, I told myself, training my mind to reflect, rather than letting the discursive mind have its way with me.

It's also not a city thing to see the effects of addiction on other beings and their families. There may be more of them here. Some of them are on the street; a lot of them are on the street. Some of them are some of the people who want money. But the point is what to do about a thing like that. Friends don't give. "What if he's going to use it to buy drugs? I would be enabling," they say.

Recently, I gave a dollar to a man on the subway who asked for it. Then I noticed that he looked high. I wondered if he thought I was a sucker. But the idea wasn't charged for me. I gave because he asked and it's a practice.

So, to not suffer is to be able to see without turning away and still incline towards kindness. And that is not to say whether to give or not to give.

Throughout towns in Asia, there are festivals that feature food and entertainment for the hungry ghosts (*pretas*). Hungry ghosts are creatures with pinhole mouths and tiny necks and huge empty stomachs that they cannot fill. Kind of the perfect personification for addiction. The festival is to honor the *pretas* and satisfy their unmet needs. It's not a perfect guide for giving. They give, not to be kind so much as so the hungry ghosts do not bring misfortune. The ghosts are also ancestors who have not been properly honored. But that's another story.

It's a question of values and seeing if I can use the moment skillfully, remembering we are not isolated. We are imbedded in a bigger space than our personal lives. It's not all about me. Perhaps I'm fortunate to have one place where my desire is not subtle. It feels like freedom to do what I want to do. But what makes me want to do what I want to do? And what about when I don't want to do something unskillful, but I do it anyway? Habits take over. But what is addiction anyway? And what forms does it take?

Craving is the arising, the wanting; clinging is the holding on, even to the desire itself, to avoid the feeling of deprivation.

The Eightfold Path deconstructs the habit patterns and offers a way through, *not around.* So, not only can I not dismiss parts of the world that seem to be too much, but I cannot dismiss parts of myself that seem to be in the way of my journey. Instead, I know they are the journey. That's why they're showing up.

> *. . . one abides . . . free from desire and discontent (longing and grief) in regards to the world.*
>
> —*SATIPATTHANA SUTTA,*
> THE FOUNDATIONS OF MINDFULNESS

The Buddha's invitation to be free from desire and discontent sounds like an order or prescription or commandment. Just stop it. Of course, not only will that not work, but pretending it will leads me to an even more dangerous place—a place of denial.

It's important to see how the mind works while we're on the cushion. But to take that into daily life—to see how the mind works in daily life—is the practice. Always looking at what the mind is doing. And knowing that what I am thinking is not entirely true (maybe not even hardly true).

So, do I stand in front of the liquor store and see how the craving feels in my body? I think not. The place to meet desire and discontent head on is on the cushion. And, in the beginning, if the craving is triggering and seducing, I'm invited to turn my attention away from the chatter of my mind to the one-pointed concentration of the breath. And if this is the kind of fear that sits with you and sits with you, and there it is again, teacher Joseph Goldstein offers two tools for dealing with fear: (1) Don't let it get even a moment's air time. If you see it coming, stop it, because, once it lands, it proliferates, and (2) Rather than struggling with the fear, ask, what if it always feels like this? Sounds odd, but it works for me.

And, I'm invited to remember that sensual pleasure is impermanent and unsatisfactory, and, when the contentment wears off, I will be left bereft and will need to want—to desire—again.

The Dhammapada teaches:

> *If, by giving up a lesser happiness,*
> *One could experience greater happiness,*
> *A wise person would renounce the lesser*
> *To behold the greater.*
>
> —*Dhammapada 290*

One more pavement practice story in New York City.

I was running and I noticed my foot on the pavement. But not just my foot on the pavement. Sometimes, even the intention to lift, to step. And then, how does the step feel? Lightness, pressure, heaviness, stiffness, heat, air. And my legs and hips and my back and my shoulders and arms, each one had their moments when they called attention to themselves. I ran and paid attention to the footfalls and the hips, and the air I was pushing through.

Sometimes I chanted. It was a long enough way that sometimes it was all a blur. I had to bring myself back to the present over and over. The present meant seeing where I was and who I was running with and what neighborhood I was running through. And the soundtrack for that neighborhood.

Somewhere in Brooklyn or Queens, they announced that the winner had crossed the finish line. I said to the runner next to me, "Anyone can run for two hours; it takes a lot to run for four and change."

When I arrived at the end of the fifteenth mile, I headed up a steep ramp to get on the Queensboro Bridge. Then I hit First Avenue and the cheers landed on my skin, my ears, my heart. Thousands of them. I wanted to cry but couldn't cry because you can't breathe and cry at the same time and I had to breathe to get through the Upper East Side, into East Harlem and over the Willis Avenue Bridge to the Bronx for the twentieth mile, where I ate jelly beans out of a little paper cup one at a time. And they were sweet fuel. And then I got to run through Harlem where people called my name even if they couldn't see my shirt and finally down Fifth Avenue and into Central Park and back out for a minute to Central Park South and then back in. Hands up.

And, it was all right. And for a little while I had everything I wanted.

AGING AND URBAN *DHAMMA* PRACTICE, NYC

by Nancy Glimm

The Buddha encouraged us to "go to the forest or the root of a tree or an empty hut" to practice. But did he mean this figuratively or literally? Is our practice an exploration in finding a peaceful and quiet place within our own minds or is that practice best achieved in the context of and in connection with a natural environment—away from manmade structures and activity? What happens to those practitioners dwelling in dense urban environments? If we are contemplating *Anicca* (impermanence), *Dukkha* (unsatisfactoriness), and *Anatta* (the absence of an abiding self), what is the difference in the urban landscape from the landscape of the country-side or forest wilderness?

This contemplation can include awareness of the aging process itself. We can bring forth the Heavenly Messengers of Sickness, Old Age, and Death for frequent recollection, and we can hold and practice with The Five Contemplations:

> *I am subject to old age; I am not exempt from old age.*
> *I am subject to illness; I am not exempt from illness.*
> *I am subject to death; I am not exempt from death.*
> *I must be parted and separated from everyone and everything dear and agreeable to me.*

I am the owner of my kamma, the heir of my kamma, I have kamma as my origin, kammas as my relative, kamma as my resort. Whatever kamma I do, good or bad, of that I shall become heir.

I remember when a dear *dhamma* friend told me she reads and contemplates the five contemplations every day. I was deeply impressed and realized they still held the sting of fear for me. Some years later now, I am feeling so appreciative of her practice, and I now frequently reflect on these five contemplations.

Bhikkhu Analayo has pointed to the positive outcomes in practice of the five contemplations: death loses its threat; it loses its dark and gloomy features. These contemplations allow our whole life to come alive and can give direction and purpose to our lives.

It may all sound so dense and heavy in the moment. But knowing our bodies are subject to the laws of nature and there is no escaping this, we can consider the body as Nature itself. And we don't need to travel to nature to practice *dhamma*; our bodies are ready to teach us. We may not need the forest.

Perhaps, the Buddha wanted us to remove ourselves from the temptations and subsequent cravings offered in urban life. But can we see clearly the craving in the mind for sense pleasure and experience, the aversion for unwanted experience, and the neutrality that allows us to gloss over so much of experience, whether we are in nature or the city?

And, while the mind meditating in the city can proliferate the desire for forests of calm, the urban landscape has other creatures, sounds, and burdens for the meditator that are equally a part of nature, just unique to the urban life. Also, today most cities offer places of refuge from stimulation—parks, sanctuaries, and more and more meditation centers.

Recently a question was posed to a meditation group I am studying with: "Have you ever meditated in nature, out of doors? What was your experience like?" It made me think of the experience of discomfort that the raw direct experience of meditating outside can create. There is the constantly changing light, temperature, the bugs, the concern for wildlife. (In California, it is the mountain lions, and in Massachusetts, it is the bears, and it's the snakes in both places). And, oh, the constant threat of ticks! I have also noticed that more and more forest retreat centers are offering climate controlled and stable retreat halls. Have you noticed this?

So, how fully have we embraced and do we live in the impermanence of our bodies, as temporary shelters, containers of our organs and all body parts? And, what about the Natural Laws of having a physical form contained in the Four Elements? We have Earth-solid, Fire-temperature, Water-liquid and Wind-motion. We are our physical construction materials, outside and inside. And outside and inside cannot be neatly separated. Separateness is an illusion, really. This is such good news. Opening wholeheartedly to the practice of our bodies as nature itself, combined with our awareness of our aging, brings urgency to practice. We can no longer fend off awareness of this natural process, this unfolding of the truth of *dhamma.*

Dhamma practice in an urban environment can sometimes show us clearly and sometimes very directly the impermanent nature of all existence. Living in NYC, down in the West Village, can be commercially packaged as lovely and exciting. Oh yes, I remember coming home on a Sunday night in 2001 from a challenging visit with a relative struggling with dementia. Driving up from the south, I remember seeing the World Trade Center all aglow. I remember commenting how wonderful it was to be safe and home! Two days later the planes struck the towers and my idea of safe home was transformed. Since that sad and tragic time, there have been other attacks of much lesser magnitude, but still causing loss of life, all around this neighborhood. The bomb that was found on the street where New York Insight Meditation Center sits just did not activate. A renowned meditation teacher asked us once at a daylong retreat, how can you live here? No one had an answer to the question. Many people just mildly shrugged their shoulders. This is a large city, we love our meditation center, we love the *dhamma*, we live here and we are subject to impermanence. Is there a better place than lower Manhattan to meditate on the Five Contemplations?

Can we see ourselves, our bodies, as a part of nature, arising, stabilizing and passing away? This is so natural, so much a part of the laws of nature. Today I contemplate the loss of a family member, someone very close to the doors of death. When will her last breath occur? I am full of feeling for her, our family matriarch. Will she be gone today, tomorrow, in two days? My heart aches also for my closest friend who will most likely not survive this year, the cancer is so aggressive.

Will I outlive them both or will an accident of some sort take me before them? When will I die? This question cannot be answered. I would like to encourage you to live in the *dhamma*; to practice; to acknowledge the great heart-opening gift of the five contemplations; to live each breath as it may be your last. Explore and investigate these beautiful teachings for yourself. Live fully and may the *dhamma* resonate in your body, heart, and mind.

KICKBOXING WITH THE *DHARMA*

by Ellen Furnari

I was very pleased to be asked to teach an introduction to *Vipassana* Buddhism at the university. I had recently moved to a city in New Zealand's south, in pursuit of a higher education degree, and knew very few people. I figured teaching would be both deeply satisfying, as it always is to share the *dharma,* and a way to connect with new people.

The class was being taught in the student union, a large three-story building. I was assigned a comfy room with some chairs and a sofa, and there were also some sitting cushions and mats available. I greeted folks as they came in; we sat down, introduced ourselves, and said a bit about our backgrounds and what we wanted from this five-week course. After a brief introduction, about which I remember nothing, I started to lead a meditation focused on breath as a way to get present, settle, and focus.

At about the same moment, music started to blare, the room rumbled from the bass, and the rhythmic thump of people jumping on the floor above (jump ropes, jumping jacks?) began in time with the rhythm of the music. It turned out that we were underneath the kickboxing studio. How exciting! What to do?

It was one of those moments in teaching when you can cry, laugh, or just make use of the moment. I must admit I was torn between the crying and laughing. But instead, I acknowledged awareness of sound and offered the invitation to notice where the mind was going—resistance to what is, the emotions arising, whatever was present. The challenge is, can we befriend whatever is in this moment? Can we not pretend this huge noise and vibration is not happening? Not get lost in the irritation, or amusement, or whatever it might be? But can we be friends with and kind to the mind that hears, that reacts, and that has opinions and views of how a meditation class is supposed to be?

Another night, when the class upstairs must have been discussing something, as there were no noises emanating from above, someone started what sounded like a car, minus muffler, in the street below. Of course, it coincided with a moment when we were meditating. Luckily, I happened to be directing people to be aware of the arising and passing of sound. These loud noises, that seemed to go on for five to ten minutes, gave us all a whole cacophony of sounds arising and changing to be aware of. Imagine how hard it would have been if it had been totally silent!

Throughout the course, there were innumerable moments to talk about being with things as they are. We want perfect conditions for meditation— if only my cushion were a bit higher, if my chair were padded, if it were quieter, darker, lighter, earlier in the day, before a meal—then surely I would achieve my desired state of a quiet mind, calm and content, and focus on whatever meditation object I have chosen.

At the beginning of each class, we each checked in, sharing about our practice in the last week. It was interesting to hear about the effects of practicing with "what is." I remember that one person spoke of their struggles to feel happier. Their understanding of positive psychology was that it was up to themselves to push the mind to feel happy with whatever was happening. The emphasis in meditation and mindfulness on acceptance of mind states was very helpful. They found it much easier to accept irritation or sadness than to try to turn it into something happy. And of course, with acceptance, the intensity of the difficulty decreased.

Between the fourth and fifth class, we also had a half-day "mini retreat" of silence—spent in sitting and walking meditation. Another person noted afterwards the depth of their connection to sights, sounds, physical movements, when walking in silence and really paying attention. This was a dramatic change from walking while also talking on the phone, listening to music, or some other simultaneous activity. They exclaimed that even the experience of urinating was so interesting, when paid attention to with mindful awareness.

In the Four Foundations of Mindfulness, or *Satipatthana Sutta,* the Buddha says: *Gone to the forest, or to the root of a tree, or to an empty hut, he sits down.* . . . Surely this is the image many of us have as the ideal setting to meditate—some place in nature, remote, quiet, empty of others, a place with no external distractions.

And it is wonderful to have such places to do sitting, walking, lying-down meditation; these kinds of environments do lend themselves to concentration.

But the teachings also point to the independence of conditions. We train to develop presence, mindfulness, awareness, connectedness with what is actually present, without judgments, in any and all conditions. If our connected, nonjudgmental awareness is dependent on quiet, on just the right seat, the right time of day, etc., then it is quite limited. So, while it would be better to teach in an environment that isn't right under the kickboxing studio (and in the next classes they gave me a lovely room removed from all that noise), our first room did provide a great opportunity to experience practice in a messy, noisy world.

Sound is, of course, not the only distraction. We can imagine that we can't meditate well, or be truly aware and awake, if we feel depressed, angry, hurt, upset, distressed, or too happy, excited, or joyful. But if not in these moments, then when? If not right now—in whatever is included in "right now"—when? And can we cultivate a kind acceptance of the full messy moment—not just accept it, but have kindness and care for ourselves and all other beings, in whatever moment we find ourselves in? This is the direction we aim for in our practice, and then we let go and see what happens: kickboxing, cars without mufflers, and all.

GROUNDED IN PRESENCE: OUR BODIES, OUR TEACHERS

by Nobantu Mpotulo

The body is our house—and how we live in it and where we occupy it are uniquely ours, as well as being part of the common human experience.—Jill Satterfield, "Meditation in Motion: How to be Present in the Body,"

—TRICYCLE MAGAZINE, 2012

How many times have you driven home from a busy day with so many things to juggle—work, personal issues, family responsibilities—and you wonder, *"How did I make it home? Who was driving the car?"* This happens to me every now and then, especially when I am not present in the moment and in my body. Being present simply means to be "Here," to be in the body moment by moment. When our attention leaves our bodies, it is then that we literally stop being present.

When I attend retreats, I find that it is easy to be present in the moment, but, unfortunately, I cannot perpetually be on retreat as our daily lives beckon us to take care of our responsibilities. In this chapter, therefore, I seek to explore means and practices that can support us to be present in the moment during our busy schedules and when the speed of life surpasses our appropriate responses.

I attended a retreat entitled "The Power of Presence in Relationships" at Dharmagiri, a retreat center in the Southern Drakensberg Mountains in KwaZulu Natal, South Africa, last year. I was struck by one of the teachers, Thanissara, saying: "The past is gone, the future is uncertain, the present is the knowing." She emphasized that we experience presence when we are in our bodies, as our bodies cannot lie. Our minds may wander and form stories that may build or break us, our hearts may respond by attaching to only pleasant feelings while having an aversion toward unpleasant feelings, but the body is always present to whatever arises and falls.

In this chapter, therefore, I share how we can utilize this ever-present body in supporting us to be present when we are thrown off center. The *Satipatthana Sutta* bears reference. When talking about The Four Postures, the Buddha said,

> *Again, monks, when walking, a monk understands 'I am walking';* *when standing, he understands 'I am standing'; when sitting, he under-* *stands 'I am sitting'; when lying down, he understands 'I am lying* *down'; or he understands accordingly however his body is disposed.*

I find that this *sutta* represents how I practice being present in my body in my line of work as an Executive Coach. Personally, and in assisting my clients to be present as well, I use a lot of practices that utilize the four postures mentioned above.

Today, I am walking through downtown Pretoria in front of the Union Building, being part of a peaceful march against violence towards women and children. I am in a sea of women and men who are saying enough is enough; we need to do something against this scourge of violence against women and children. Normally I experience a sense of discomfort in crowded areas, but I decided to be part of this march because of what it represents.

This particular march was sparked by a femicide where a male partner killed and burnt the body of his partner, a twenty-two-year-old woman. The march is under the title #NotInMyName that is organized by men in response to #MenAreTrash, which was coined by women against the latest violations of women in South Africa. A report by the Medical Research Council asserts that 45.6 percent of women in Africa experience physical and sexual violence, compared to 35 percent worldwide.

As I march amongst the hundreds of marchers, I start to feel sensations in my body. I feel a tight knot in my stomach, and as I continue to listen to my body, I start to shake; my body is reacting to the latest violence against women resulting in sexual and physical attacks. I notice a sudden tingling in my legs. I allow myself to practice mindfulness amongst the masses and to be fully present with what I am feeling and sensing in my body. I suddenly notice a tightening in my chest and sadness engulfs me as I reflect on the many lives of women lost by the hands of their partners or whoever the perpetrators are. As I start to allow the feelings to rise, I experience a relaxation in my body; the vibrations of the crowds around me have a calming effect on my body; I start to experience a slowing down in my heartbeat, and I become one with the other people around me, both the alleged victims and the alleged perpetrators of violence against women and children.

Part of the poem *Please Call Me by My True Names* by Thich Nhat Hanh comes into my mind:

> *I still arrive, in order to laugh and to cry,*
> *to fear and to hope,*
> *the rhythm of my heart is the birth and death*
> *of all that are alive.*
>
> *I am the twelve-year-old girl,*
> *refugee on a small boat,*
> *who throws herself into the ocean*
> *after being raped by a sea pirate.*
> *And I am the pirate,*
> *my heart not yet capable*
> *of seeing and loving.*
>
> *Please call me by my true names,*
> *so I can hear all my cries and laughter at once,*
> *so I can see that my joy and pain are one.*

As I become present in my body and allow this poem to be my teacher, I soon realize that, even as a woman, I am both a victim and a perpetrator. I soon experience a grounded state and I notice tears running down my face. A realization comes to my mind that seeing just one side is polarizing, but when I see myself on both sides, I move away from pointing fingers at others. And I also enlist to become part of the solution.

This experience brings to my mind how some of the practices I use to be present involve walking meditation and becoming aware of sensations in the different parts of the body, from the sensations on the soles of my feet as they touch the ground, the sensations my breath causes around my nostrils, the pulse of my heart as I am breathing in and out. As I become fully in this practice today in this march, I find that it connects me fully to all parts of me, and it also connects me to the people I am marching alongside.

I also use mindfulness practices when I go to the municipal offices to renew the license for my car. I get to the offices as early as 7 am, and as I near the entrance, I notice there is already a long queue. As soon as I see the queue, I realize that it is going to be a long wait. When this thought hits my mind, I notice an internal conversation in my head that goes: *You know, you can go and come back another time.* Another voice comes and says: *Well, even if you come back another time there will still be a long queue.* As the second voice comes, I notice some frustration and anger welling up, and I hear another voice starting to blame how inefficient our government is, and I begin to conceptualize how to suggest systems for improvement.

At about 7:45 am the queue starts to move a little bit, and a sense of hope starts to emerge. A smile starts to form, I feel a slight twitch on my lips, and I start to relax and enjoy the sensations on my lips. In this blissful state I hear some shouting, and I strain my neck to see where that is coming from. Well, someone was trying to jump the queue and other people are not hearing of it. I start to realize that I am not the only one who feels frustrated here.

This realization makes me aware that others too are suffering like I am. I start to pay attention to the soles of my feet as I am standing. I move my toes slightly and become acutely aware of the movement. I move the toes in the other foot. I move from my toes up to my ankles with renewed awareness and paying attention to the sensations. I continue to go through all different joints in my body. I move to my torso, chest, and head, and become aware of what is arising. I experience some relaxation and I notice that I am now closer and closer to the counters. I notice a flutter in my chest cavity; yes, there is some excitement there.

After two hours, I emerge on the other side, the side with an EXIT sign. Bravo. I have survived the ordeal. I start to thank my body and tell it that I will remember next time that the body is an ever-present teacher.

I do remember. But the lessons are hard, and fear precludes us all from being present.

I remember one experience in September 2015, when I decided to face one of my fears head on. This is a fear I have had from when I was a child—the fear of heights. As a child, I could not even go down a slide; this would literally paralyze me and cause me difficulty breathing. Brave me decided that in my fifties I was ready to face this fear, and guess what I decided to do? I decided to go bungee jumping from the highest bridge in Africa (about 220 meters, or 722 feet), the Bloukrans Bridge in Tsitsikama, South Africa. I went in the morning with two friends, but my fear succeeded in stopping me from jumping. I went back in the afternoon as the encouragement from my friends would not let me back down.

I finally made the jump.

And I have never experienced such fear in my life. As I opened my eyes, being suspended from a rope, I saw below a big river, the Bloukrans River, with dark slimy water. The sky was farther and farther up above me. All I had was me and my fear. When this realization came through, I became aware of my ever-present body and closed my eyes, focusing on deep breathing. I started to notice my knotted tummy starting to relax, my heart starting to relax; I experienced a stillness I have never experienced in my life. I became one with nature, and I felt a great sense of gratitude. A pool of tears started to run down my cheeks joining in with the murky waters below me. This was a true experience of being present in CONQUERING my worst fear. In our busy lives, be it at work or walking down a busy street amongst the crowds, we are confronted with so many fears. It is through being present in our bodies that we can overcome these fears.

Some of the other places that make us fearful are our workspaces. I notice often when I am about to make a pitch to a potential client, to make a presentation in a conference, or when having a chemistry session with a coaching client, I always experience immense fear, which makes me want to run away. The fleeing from the task at hand normally is linked to the stories in my head that might go like this: *the people will not like my presentation, the prospective client will think that I am not good enough, who the heck am I fooling, I cannot do this.* All these thoughts and stories start to make me want to run away or I will freeze. When this happens, I notice my body—my palms start to sweat, my legs feel wobbly, my heart beats faster, and I feel a closing of my throat as if my voice will not be clearly projected. When I acknowledge these reactions in my body, I find that I become like a willow tree with its branches swaying from side to side uncontrollably in a gust of wind.

My calm gets restored when I start to breathe deeply in, filling my lungs and stomach, and gently breathe out, and this continued deep breathing in and out starts to relax me. Standing in a warrior's stance and feeling the ground supporting me also makes the fear subside, and as I walk mindfully towards the object of my fear, paying attention to what happens in my body, slowly I get grounded and my presence is restored.

These experiences are always there to remind me that the body is my ever-present teacher, support, and friend never to be doubted and undermined.

In looking at presence from a work perspective, I know I'm not alone, and I asked some of my fellow coaches how they identify and cultivate presence.

Thabiso Baloyi: *My "signature presence" can be identified by the state of contagious calmness that I tend to bring to my surroundings and anybody who happens to be in my company.*

Colin Adam: *When I have embodied Presence, I experience a feeling of being in my body, which equates to a calm centeredness. This gives me the ability to choose my responses rather than to react, and to have a feeling of well-being, strength, and influence.*

Conroy Fourie: *Presence is essentially about leadership through influence, the authentic use of power, by a leader with high self-awareness and high emotional intelligence.*

Ladina King: *Presence is a moment in time, where I am released from my fixations and habits. In that moment, I am present to what is in front of me, I am not attached to anything, I am in flow with what is.*

Adelle Wapnick: *My "signature presence" lies in a tension between intellect and humor. I am an ambivert, so there is tension between quietness (intellect) and engagement (humor).*

These shared experiences remind me that the body is my ever-present teacher, support, and friend, never to be doubted or undermined.

SANGHA, LOVE

ANGER IS A MESSENGER

by JD Doyle

"What about anger? All I feel is anger at the injustice," a twentyish, white, gender non-conforming person voiced at the end of our Friday evening meditation. My co-teacher and I were finishing an evening on forgiveness, as she had just returned from a month-long retreat where the practice of forgiveness had brought her powerful insight. And yet, this question, the question of anger, had arisen. How does one navigate the terrain of forgiveness in a world built on historical injustices and day-to-day acts of discrimination and prejudice?

I am grateful when I receive this question about the role of anger. And it happens fairly regularly at the East Bay Meditation Center (EBMC), which was "*founded to provide a welcoming environment for people of color, members of the LGBTQI community, people with disabilities, and other underrepresented communities.*" So many of us have been marginalized, discriminated against, excluded, and othered, and carry legacies of pain and wounding. Many of us have moved to the city, to Oakland, and shown up at EBMC, in search of acceptance, in search of understanding, and in search of love.

The lure of the possibilities that exist in the city—the diversity, the opportunities, the multiplicity of cultures—converge to create rich fertile ground to breathe one's self into being, an existence that moves beyond tolerance to celebration. Within the spectrum of cultures, genders, races, a white gender-queer person like myself may receive the occasional slight, but not open hostility, or being overlooked or ignored. Within this rich, vibrant city the whole of the *dharma* is revealed and the whole of my being can find home.

One of the most notable stories of the Buddha is of the four heavenly messengers. After living royally in gated and secluded areas where the vicissitudes of life were kept at bay, the Buddha-to-be ventured out into the village. In the streets of the village, he was startled, upset, and troubled by what he witnessed—a sick person, an old person, and a dead person. In the story, the sight of these people, these messengers, awakened him from the trance of acting from his habitual patterns. The fourth heavenly messenger was a wandering monk, whose radiant countenance awakened him to the possibility of a path to freedom.

This quality of awakening, called in Pali *samvega*, is a sense of urgency. According to monk and teacher Bhikku Bodhi, it is *"an inner commotion or shock which does not allow us to rest content with our habitual adjustment to the world. Instead it drives us on, out of our cozy palaces and into unfamiliar jungles, to work out with diligence an authentic solution to our existential plight."*

And so, when the question of anger arises at EBMC, I welcome it and share how anger has been a messenger in my life. When I feel the rise of anger in my body, I pay attention. I pause, I inquire: *What is calling forth this emotion, this energy?* I pay attention, not only to the sensations in the body, but also to the ways that anger can point to norms or attitudes that promulgate injustice, exclusivity, and harm.

Bhikkhu Bodhi calls out the traditional legendary old person, the sick person, and the corpse as gods in disguise, spurs to awakening. My messengers are also spurs to awakening, rather than something to be eliminated or gotten rid of. Instead, when anger arises, I view that as an invitation to turn towards the experience rather than look away.

I have practiced in many meditation centers, where the atmosphere and surroundings confine everyone to binary gender rules and emphasize the dominant white culture. For example, at a rural retreat center, I remember my surprise at finding out that the extra supply of clothes for cold weather was organized by gender: sweaters, jackets, and hats deemed suitable for men labeled and stacked on one side of the shelves, and those for women on the other. I questioned the necessity for this dichotomy and wondered why clothing had to have a gender. And, I admit that in looking for a scarf to keep warm, I was by maddened by the imposition of binary cultural norms. Over the years, I have used anger to help guide me to places like EBMC, where we are creating radically inclusive spaces for all people.

At the front of most meditation halls, including at EBMC, there is a statue of the Buddha, his pose serene; often this image is translated to mean that we too, should be serene, calm, and unmoved by all that surrounds us—untouched and untroubled. And yet . . . the statues of the Buddha are after his enlightenment. On the Buddha's journey to enlightenment, he encountered fear, hatred, craving, and confusion. The serenity of the Buddha statues can lead us to forget all the ups and downs of his journey. And the singular figure we see in most statues can lead us to forget that he went out into the community to teach. Community surrounded him and he taught from that place.

At the East Bay Meditation Center, we have created another altar that honors and acknowledges "Black Lives Matter." This altar is covered with photos of loved ones lost to violence, to police brutality, to old age, to sickness, and to struggle. The altar is a call to remembrance, a testimony to love, and a reminder of the legacies of anger and rage that many members of our community feel. In highlighting the brutality of the systems and institutions of oppression in which we live, our community includes them as part of our spiritual practice. In *sangha*, in community, we can be held in the hearts of each other, while we work with the histories of anger, rage, and despair. It is a long, arduous practice.

For me this is where practicing in diverse *sanghas* is essential. Like the countenance of the fourth messenger, the diverse community of practitioners helps provide inspiration and refuge. When I think or act solely as an individual from my own frame of reference, the plight of humanity feels Sisyphean. When community comes together intentionally, the interaction between diverse cultures, many languages, different understandings of the world, and myriad ways of knowing, the possibilities for freedom are increased exponentially.

As I open to the amazing diversity of humanity, my unconscious habit patterns and cultural conditioning are revealed. As a white practitioner, part of my practice is to commit to learning and trying to understand the complex violence of this country's histories and my own history within this context. This inquiry plays a critical part to understanding myself and to transforming the energies of anger into liberatory practice. When I face anger, I increase my ability to understand our connectedness and to learn and to let go of conditioned habits that are no longer skillful.

On my way to and from EBMC, I pass under the freeways where the homeless encampments have been growing steadily: a makeshift city of tents, tarps, beds, couches, pallets, and a multitude of people. One evening, as I bike home from EBMC, I notice an older black man preparing his bed on the sidewalk: a white sheet spread out fastidiously over a mattress, the sheet turned down, hotel style, with a pillow placed in the center. It is an alarmingly intimate moment, his life on the stage (on the side of the street). I'm struck by the contradiction of his loving attention to his abode with the lack of attention and care for those who are homeless. I feel the complexity of the situation in my heart, as both beautiful and deadly, as I have seen the statistics of what happens to those who are homeless in Oakland. As I pedal my bike home, I notice the anger arising in my body. Then the complexity of emotions ensues—compassion, despair, sadness, and love in my body. And I am moved. I am moved to expand my notion of acceptability beyond that of my white middle class upbringing. I am moved to turn toward the anger, listen to the wisdom of the body, and practice with this complexity both internally and in community.

Over the twenty years of my practice, I have heard and read many times of the need to control anger; that one needs to curb one's anger and "not allow this feeling to reside in our minds." I am curious as to how anger has been emphasized in our Buddhist circles as something to eliminate and to restrain, rather than to ponder and open to the stories it can share. It is a challenge to speak in the *dharma* hall about actions in the larger society that create suffering. Some Buddhists ask if it is an appropriate and necessary part of our practice. And it is a challenge to take responsibility for actions within the *sangha* that create suffering. None of us is immune from acting unskillfully. Despite good intentions, our cultural conditioning and ignorance often result in blunders and harm. What happens when my actions anger another? Is there room for *sangha* to say unwise things and to learn from each other? Diverse communities provide many opportunities to address the sufferings that occur in the larger society. And address them we must. This is the sense of urgency that can arise if we are open to it.

My practice has increased my ability to hold the complexity of experiences that come with anger and to not need to fix it right away to get rid of the suffering. First, knowing that suppression, repression, and avoidance lead to the dangerous place of denial. It takes pause and awareness.

translated as "clarity and serene confidence." According to Thanissaro Bhikkhu, "It is what keeps *samvega* from turning into despair. In the prince's case, he gained a clear sense of his predicament and of the way out of it, leading to something beyond aging, illness, and death, at the same time feeling confident that the way would work." *Pasada* is also translated as "faith," which inherently connects the urge to awaken to the heart. This combination of the head and heart reflects the embodied wisdom that anger offers to us if we don't turn away from it.

I feel lucky to practice in a community that does not ignore anger. While it isn't always easy, and it requires patience, forbearance, loving-kindness, and compassion, I am opening to the stories that anger brings me. Anger reminds me deeply to pause, to reflect, and reconnect. So, when I hear others bring up the question of anger, their own or others, I am grateful, for I know a rich conversation will ensue, one that will awaken us to our community, to our ancestors, and to the interconnected web in which we all live. The messages of awakening that anger can give us provide us with a path toward freedom. Rather than dismiss the jolt of awareness that accompanies anger, can we experience it as a reminder of our connection to others and to our commitment to love?

THE PERFECTION OF COMMUNITY

by Rachel Lewis

Retreat is a powerful form of meditation practice. Dropping interaction means dropping habit patterns around interaction, and instead exploring what it means to be present in the moment in a straightforward way. During my first three-month retreat, I enjoyed expansive feelings of open-heartedness. I felt excited as I started wondering whether I had permanently shifted into a more patient, kind way of being in the world. When I got back to my ordinary life, though, I was dismayed to find how quickly patterns of impatience and irritation reasserted themselves. I've come to see that there's a form of purification of heart and mind that can happen only in community.

The Zen teacher Seung Sahn says that when people wash potatoes in Korea, instead of washing them one at a time they put them all in a tub full of water. Then someone plunges a stick into the tub, stirring the potatoes around so they rub together, knocking the dirt off one another. In that way, the potatoes become clean. Similarly, when we're bumping up against other people's rough edges and irritating tendencies, we see our own problem areas in a different way than we do in the seclusion of retreat.

We have the opportunity to choose different ways of relating to our difficulties: to see them primarily as fuel for practice, and to evaluate ourselves more on the sincerity of our effort to purify the heart than on whether or not external conditions are the way we want them to be. The principles that guide this exploration are summarized in the Buddhist list of the *paramis*—the qualities of heart that spiritual seekers perfect over long lifetimes of practice.

Giving—*Dana*

Giving is a foundational practice in many spiritual traditions, and Buddhism is no exception. The power of giving is the first step of the Buddha's teaching. Through seemingly simple acts of sharing, we cultivate qualities like generosity and goodwill for others, and we also loosen the bonds of greed and attachment by seeing what we can do without. Generosity is a beautiful motivation for giving. It flows naturally when the heart feels a sense of connection, but generosity and connection can also arise from the act of giving itself.

For several years, I was one of a handful of people responsible for taking care of the practicalities of running an open sitting group: I would have to show up at the same time each week to unlock the door and set out cushions. Some weeks it very much felt like something I had to do, rather than something I was doing because my heart was overflowing with generosity, but what I noticed was that repeated acts of generosity—with my time and attention, in this case—led to a feeling of closeness and warmth for the group I was taking care of.

Once there's a sense of belonging and appreciation in the group, it's really natural to share freely—bringing home-cooked food to gatherings, helping members find jobs and housing, helping members with chores and errands in times of need. In this individualistic culture, the act of giving is countercultural—as is asking for help!

I've had some great conversations with friends while I was doing their dishes, during times when they weren't able to do them themselves.

As the quality of generosity develops and grows, it becomes more expansive, reflecting good will for people who are not part of any group that you feel an affinity for. That might manifest as taking actions to protect everyone's access to clean water and air, education, and health care. Generosity as a spiritual practice cannot be separated from its political dimension!

Integrity—*Sila*

Acting with integrity is another form of generosity. When we are consistent about acting with integrity, we offer the gift of safety to the people around us. Integrity is a form of lovingkindness, because we wish our actions to promote the well-being of everyone we interact with, and also of wisdom, in two ways: because of the understanding that our actions do have consequences, and because of the understanding that no happiness that depends on the unhappiness of others can be stable and satisfying. Embodying integrity means being consistent about speaking truthfully and harmlessly, and about acting kindly and consistently.

Within meditation groups, sometimes there's a conflict between the desire to be open and welcoming to all newcomers while also being safe for everyone and particularly for those who experience multiple oppressions in everyday life. Coming up with community guidelines that are conducive to safety is a challenge that's very much alive for many of us.

Renunciation—*Nekkhamma*

Renunciation can sound off-putting at first—nobody wants to miss out on fun things!—but it's another key part of developing these perfections. Renunciation can mean simplicity: having fewer things going on in your life so that you can bring a better quality of presence to the things you're most committed to. In meditation, we practice renouncing the desire to be elsewhere, over and over again, so we can bring our full attention to where we actually are at the moment.

It can also mean an attitude shift: renouncing being the star of the show, as Philip Moffitt would say. It's as if you're changing the camera angle from one that's focused on you as an individual to one that takes in the whole group. This kind of renunciation can enable you to engage with the people around you in a more openhearted way, seeing their needs as individuals as being as important as your own. Giving up the need to have everything be about you all the time is a relief!

Wisdom—*Panna*

Wisdom is what arises when you're in contact with the truth of the moment. It's this knowledge through experience that can arise in each of us when we are seeing clearly how things really are right now. For me, wisdom is summed up in something my teacher has said to me many times: "How about you just let things be the way they are?"

This showed up in my life in a painful way in a situation where I tried to force a friendship to develop. I'd met somebody who shared many of my interests, and it seemed like it should be a natural fit for us to spend time together and perhaps work together on projects. It took me a long time to realize that this person just wasn't as interested as I was in getting these projects off the ground. "How about you just let this relationship be the way it is?" Not all relationships are going to evolve the way you hope, but it is in relationship with each other, bumping up against the ways that we disappoint or perplex each other, that we learn to see through our ideas about how things should be, all the way to how they actually are at the moment.

Energy—*Viriya*

Sometimes people are surprised to see energy on a Buddhist list. The idea in popular culture is that meditation is always about relaxing. It's true that in our overstimulated culture it's valuable to learn to relax, but some degree of energy is always necessary. The wise use of energy means using just enough—not too much, not too little—to stay present.

For many of us, that means learning where we over-use energy (through perfectionism and workaholism) as a distraction from other things that need our attention.

It might also mean using energy to follow through on our intentions, even if that's as simple as meditating every day or showing up for a meditation group every week. A friend of mine had a solid meditation practice at home, but had mental blocks about joining a group. When he found a group that he was interested in joining, he had to work hard to talk himself into going to the first session. Seeing how good he felt afterwards made it a bit easier for him to talk himself into the second session. Over the course of a few months, it got much easier for him to leave his comfort zone in this way. Applying energy to do something that was important to him led to him feeling inspired and energized, rather than drained.

Patience—*Khanti*

Patience has sometimes been called long-enduring mind: being willing to keep trying even when it doesn't seem like anything good is happening. The Buddha also called it the supreme virtue, which I sometimes think of as the enabling virtue, meaning that being willing to stay with things long enough to see their nature is what enables wisdom to arise.

Patience is also related to renunciation: renouncing the demands that we all tend to make of the universe—about how things should be right now. Of all the *paramis*, this is the one that you'll inevitably end up practicing in community!

Even something as simple as a friend expressing interest in meditation and then not showing up to events—what's the response to that? It's a practice of patience to just keep sharing information when they ask, without getting attached to them actually following through on their intentions.

Truthfulness—*Sacca*

Many of us struggle in one way or another with truthfulness. For some, the struggle is to limit ourselves to saying only what's true—giving up the habit of exaggerating for comic effect, for example.

For others, the struggle is in the willingness to speak up about what's true in our experience at the moment.

There's a related challenge around being willing to make room for what's true for other people. This could be as simple as making space for other people's truth in group discussions—taking in life experiences that are different from your own.

It can also mean the willingness to take in uncomfortable truths about others you wish to think well of.

Resolve—*Adhitthana*

Resolve is the determination that helps you follow through on your intentions. It can be as simple as committing to show up for community events even when your energy is low: Resolve is persistence in aligning yourself with what you know is wise.

Persistence has to be balanced by patience and by wisdom. Some of us have too much resolve! I spent several years in a career that wasn't a good match for me or my interests. I found myself in a job interview hearing my own lackluster answers and realizing that what the conversation boiled down to was, "Tell me why you want this job," and me saying, "Actually I don't."

It was only in that interview that I realized that persistence had become unbalanced in my life: that I kept on going just because I'd started out in a particular direction. Once I saw clearly that there was no wisdom in this persistence, I was able to let go of my attempts to make myself into something I honestly didn't really want to be and to change direction in my professional life.

Kindness—*Metta*

Coming into community gives us a chance to test the quality of our good will. In retreat, we have a beautiful opportunity to cultivate boundless lovingkindness. Coming out of retreat, we get a chance to see how that goodwill stands up to the foibles of the people around us. Can I see the humanity of people I disagree with, or people who are irritating? Can I keep an open heart even when I need to set boundaries?

The Buddha said that a community will endure and thrive when members cultivate good will for each other in their thoughts, words, and actions, both in public and private. This means sincerity: not saying nice things to people's faces while criticizing them behind their backs.

It also means straightforward appreciation without an agenda, rather than sexual objectification. Nothing tears a group apart faster than romantic relationships gone wrong! Freedom from romantic entanglements is more realistic in a monastic setting than among lay folk, but it's worth having some boundaries around which relationships are acceptable within the community: having teachers, at least, be scrupulous about maintaining simple good will for their students. Offering students the gifts of safety and of freedom from objectification is an important ingredient for trust to exist within the community.

Equanimity—*Upekkha*

Equanimity means finding ease in the midst of life's ups and downs. It's the spaciousness of heart that can stay present with difficulties without getting overwhelmed by them. Sometimes I think of it as a grandparent's love: a deep caring, but without the tendency of new parents to panic at every little thing that happens to their child.

When I was very young, my best friend and I used to like to play games where we would be characters from our favorite movies and TV shows, and make up elaborate stories about the adventures we were having. When we saw the first Star Wars movie, we both wanted to play Princess Leia in our stories. My friend kept telling me that I couldn't be Princess Leia; I had to be Chewbacca. I didn't want to be Chewbacca. Our argument turned into a screaming fight. My father came in to try to figure out what was going on. Instead of getting involved in our argument or trying to convince us that we shouldn't argue, he just sat with one arm around each of us as we sobbed with rage until gradually we calmed down. His simple caring presence in that moment is a touchstone for equanimity for me, almost forty years later.

The perfection of practice

If we're really honest with ourselves, many of us will admit that we come to meditation hoping that these techniques will surround us with an impenetrable bubble that will buffer us from all of life's disappointments—that we'll float through life on a plane exalted above the mundane world of irritating roommates, inconsiderate coworkers, and impatient fellow drivers. The gift of the *paramis* is the recognition that everything in life can be part of practice: that the cultivation of these mental qualities is something that we can undertake no matter how frustrating the external circumstances. Taking on the practice of cultivating the *paramis* can be powerful because it entails a shift of perspective: from one in which outer success (achieving your objectives, getting recognition, having conditions be pleasant) is of the highest importance, to one in which you evaluate yourself on how consistently you're staying true to your intentions to act with kindness, wisdom, and generosity. This shift of perspective in itself is a kind of freedom.

May we all wake up in the midst of everything!

AWAKENING IN NEW YORK CITY

by Rosemary Blake

One of our family stories is that when I was twelve years old, apropos of nothing my mother could identify, I announced that I was going to be awake this time. I had no idea what that meant and neither did my mom, but I knew to follow the strong urge to speak the words aloud. She accepted it as another strange thing her youngest child would say and then took my words as license to stand outside my room running the vacuum cleaner at 7:00 am on Saturday mornings, the day I relished sleeping until noon.

It took decades before my declaration "to be awake this time" showed up. I had long since rejected the religion of my family and community, given up teaching Sunday School, attending the eleven o'clock service, singing in the choir, and all the rest, in favor of seeing myself as a spiritual being, a seeker on a spiritual path with an intention to be awake this life-time both to what life really is and what it has to offer. Not just to my thoughts and illusions.

As an adult, I experienced the mind as a tyrant and often felt oppressed by the unending deluge of thought formations that sometime entertained but more often occurred as distractions. My meditation practice helped somewhat, but I knew something else was available. On my birthday fourteen years ago I remembered what I told my mom and wondered when I was going to "get started." and within a few weeks the Buddha, the *Dharma* and the *Sangha* showed up.

Walking meditation

I live in New York City, a town of pedestrians moving, striding down avenues in sneakers or heels, riding scooters or cycles, trains or buses, at all hours. From my first steps at nine months old, walking has been a grand adventure. Now I have walking in the city as a *Vipassana* meditation practice that's expanded the adventure. It has me fully occupying both this body and this moment. Aware of seeing, hearing, touching, feeling, thinking, moving, whatever is here NOW.

As a New Yorker, getting around the city is often about arriving unscathed at the destination as quickly as possible, darting through an obstacle course of bodies, bicycles, strollers, carts, skateboards, taxis, cars, and buses, to name a few, to say nothing of tourists strolling with skyward gaze, pausing every few steps to take yet another picture. It occurred to me that the first quality I would fully awaken to was impatience.

How to be awake and aware during a significant part of the day as I moved around town was the conundrum I took to my teacher. He gave me a technique that was like candy to the mind and would accommodate my normal walking pace.

It was unlike the walking meditation technique I first learned. Walking at a slow gait, attentive to the movement of the thighs, legs, and feet, breaking down the elements of an activity I mastered decades ago into its component parts—silently noting the lifting, moving, and placing of every footstep for twenty or so paces, then pausing, turning around, and doing the same thing in the opposite direction—seemed unimaginable on the streets of Manhattan! What was bliss in the stillness of nature at a silent meditation retreat center or in the privacy of my apartment was ill-advised for my "normal" life.

I learned to assign a number to each step at the moment my foot touches the ground—Thich Nhat Hanh describes it as caressing the earth, a satisfying image—first counting one, two, three, four, five steps. Then one, two, three, four, five, six steps, followed by one, two, three, four, five, six, seven steps, always going back to one and adding a number to the end of each sequence until I reach ten steps. That's one cycle. Then it begins again, with *five* steps, then six . . . ending with *ten* steps and repeating for as long as I am walking. If at any point a thought, a sight, a sound, or any other visitor to the sense doors distracts my attention and I lose track of my place in the counting sequence, I know my mind has segued to a place other than the movement of my body. In that moment, just like bringing attention back to the breath when I realize I'm lost in thoughts or sensations while in sitting meditation, I bring full attention back to the body moving through space with awareness as I begin counting again, the first five steps, followed by six steps, etc., to see if I can get to the end of the cycle without losing concentration. Simple, but not easy.

This practice meant I could meditate everywhere, leaving my apartment, going to and from the subway, on errands in the neighborhood, anywhere, everywhere these feet take me. The Buddha said there are four meditation positions, sitting, walking, standing, and lying down. The experience of being awake and aware moment to moment, during an ever-greater part of my day, occurred as a gift.

My first reaction was to double down and have the moving and counting be the intense focus of my walking meditation until I built up enough concentration to stay grounded there. Then I surmised I would be able to entertain thoughts without fear of being lost to the present moment. I decided to engage only with thoughts that pertain to things occurring in the "now" as added insurance. *"Ah, that beautiful tree." "Watch out, someone didn't pick up after their dog."* A present-moment marriage of seeing and thinking. Then I moved from trying to banish most thoughts, to noticing thinking as it occurred, irrespective of content. That took the practice to another level.

I discovered something about this mind in the new walking practice: it loves rhythms and counting. In my walks through the city streets I could walk, count, see, hear, and have thoughts arise in what appeared to be the same moment. This mind is often engaged in counting or performing calculations internally, acts that do not require all my attention. There is something about the rhythm of walking, like music, that my body responds to, which, when added to the rhythm of the counted numbers, is quieting, joyful, and calming. It gently engages the thought process and my attention is free to align with the moving, shifting awareness in a very open natural way. I relish this open awareness. With a quieted mind I can feel the foot lifting and moving and placing to caress the earth, the muscles in my body contracting to have that occur, the air sweeping across my cheek as the train enters the station, the leaves rustling in the oak tree at the subway entrance, and the thumping of wheels against concrete and metal as the passenger in a plaid jacket pulls her luggage to the exit. When not lost in thought I am aware of all of this and more, mindful of the many things that occur for this body to experience. This came as a great surprise.

There are a number of ways I've learned to bring myself to the present moment: Asking, *What are you listening to now? What's happening now?* Taking three deep breaths. But walking the streets of Manhattan awake and aware, that is bliss.

Self compassion

Compassion is a very important element of a meditation practice in general, and compassion for one's self is especially important. It is difficult inside the success/failure paradigm so prevalent in a city like New York to have a practice, to have techniques like listening and being with the breath, or being with the present moment and concentrating, when you are habitually judging yourself. Most of the moments will not be "successful" the way most of us define success—especially at the beginning of practice. So, kindness and self-compassion are essential. So is recognizing that the mind will wander.

One of the reasons I find the city to be a perfect place to practice being awake moment to moment is the sheer density of opportunities to meet myself and my reactions. Compassion plays an important part because many of the reactions are unpleasant and if I want to think of myself as a spiritual being on the path to a life of skillful means and wise intention, I must include the reactions of the judging mind. The moment I walk out the door, I'm surrounded by human beings, human energy, people paying attention to their cell phones rather than where they are going, people jostling each other, crossing my path and cutting me off, and so much more. How do I meet each of these moments? What do I bring to them? Can I meet and engage each one as it is, adding nothing? Sometimes I can and sometimes I can't. But each encounter provides the opportunity to see what is arising in the moment, regardless of whether or not I like what I find. Kindness and compassion for self and others are qualities that support the intention to be with whatever shows up, including those unskillful reactions I may later regret. Each time I walk out the door there is an opportunity to practice being a mindful human being.

Finding sanctuary

I can now smile about the experience of living in a physical space that I love and created as a beautiful sanctuary and then experiencing construction in the apartments above and across from me, in the grounds outside the building, and in the surrounding area for more than two years. My quiet, bucolic little neighborhood became very noise-filled. It did not make me happy. My initial reaction was annoyance, followed by accommodation, that escalated to anger, and then rage by the third month. It was interesting to notice the appearance of those strong emotions and my attendant misery, until I recognized their utter uselessness in a situation over which I have no control.

At some point I remembered a teaching of Ajahn Chah, the renowned and venerated Thai Forest monk, who gave an example of the suffering many of us experience in relation to the thought formations of the mind. He said, "Suppose you go and sit in the middle of a freeway with the cars and trucks charging down at you. You can't get angry at the cars, shouting, 'Don't drive over here!' You can't tell them that. It's a freeway. So what can you do? You get off the road!" The road is the place where cars run; if you don't want the cars to be there, you suffer.

With respect to sound, he gave an example of being disturbed by a sound when meditating, saying, "We think, 'Oh, that sound's bothering me' and we suffer accordingly . . . If we investigate a little deeper, we will see that it's we who go out and disturb the sound! The sound is simply sound. If we understand like this then there's nothing more to it, we leave it be."

I first experienced the truth of this while traveling with a close friend who knew of my morning meditation and, as she put it, had been "trained" to be completely silent. An "untrained" friend joined us one morning and the two began conversing in normal tones. I was livid. In a huff, I grabbed my blanket and pillows, sat under the windowsill and wrapped myself in the drapes so I could have the "quiet" required to mediate. I sat there fuming and fussing mentally, completely consumed with how wrong and inconsiderate they were, and whatever else the mind came up with. Until the moment when I realized the noise in my head was the loudest sound in the room. I was all I could hear.

When I recalled this teaching, my experience of the construction shifted. I stopped going out disturbing the sound or engaging with the mind's complaints and emotional reactions. Instead, as the Buddha taught, I went back to mindfulness of the body. Because even with the sounds around me, the breath was still coming in and going out, the heart was still beating, I could feel the silky texture of the rug under my feet, my thighs resting on the chair, the muscle cramp forming in my shoulder. I could follow my awareness there once I was willing to let "noise" be sound.

I now say I can meditate anywhere. That's when I remember what I know. I ask myself, "What am I listening to moment to moment?" Am I listening to the never-ending comments on reality as created by this mind? Or am I listening to the breath and what is there in present moment awareness? That space of stillness is not dependent on external circumstances. It is available when I place my attention on the place where stillness resides. That's been the biggest teaching so far.

Sangha and connection

I had never heard the word *sangha* until I encountered the Buddhist path. Looking back, I realize that I have always collected "*sanghas*"—the community of like-minded spirits to engage with, support, and be supported by. And one of the things about the proclivity to be in community, to be in *sangha*, is that an urban experience, especially the NY experience, offers one a wide range to choose from. The brilliance of *sangha* is the proximity and support of people who are traveling the same path, seeking the same surcease of suffering, grief, and lamentation and the truth of how it is, really. They can mirror the ten thousand joys and ten thousand sorrows of the human experience.

The thing that I love about being an urban creature is that all of my passions have communities that offer support—whether it's the *dharma*, engaging in the arts to educate and inspire, or empowering people to identify and manifest their vision for the black community and the world. There is nothing quite like that. With ease I find expression for the things that are meaningful, that have value, and can do so with an open heart. That's what the practice has provided—the ability to be here openheartedly rather than inside the throes of the comparative or judging mind. To come from the space of . . . *What if the Buddha and truth is speaking through that really annoying human being standing in front of me? Like a possibility?* It alters my ability to listen and to learn.

Teaching

One of my favorite teaching commitments is the aging *sangha* at my meditation center that began as a five-week class that became a weekly gathering for the *sangha* to continue their exploration of the role of a spiritual practice on the aging process. It was a surprise to discover how elated people were to have a place where they could talk about this very important aspect of their lives. Each week we come together to meditate, offer the wisdom of the *dharma*, and uncover our own wisdom in discussion. And while there are three of us who alternate teaching weekly, my interest was to find a feminine perspective to aging, one that acknowledges both the joys and sorrows.

In the beginning the sharing in the room was about loss, lack, the inability to do what used to be the norm, physical deterioration, and anticipation of additional loss. It is amazing to be engaged in an investigation of what is available in a time that is held as negative and painful. We've discovered that our view of the truth depends on *how* we're holding whatever is in front of us. Whether we are eighteen, thirty, fifty, seventy, or eighty-five, we're all aging. It only becomes significant when we begin to look at ourselves as "old," in a state of inevitable decline, or, as the Buddha discovered, when we engage with the three heavenly messengers of aging, sickness, and death. The engagement is so rich. The *sangha* has bonded even as new people appear each week. And we learn not only from the teachings but from our shared experience and reactions. We get to watch each other shift, change, and grow. We're always changing. But in this space we can acknowledge the beauty and encounter the truth of living with impermanence, which includes acceptance of what is and the beginner's mind for what's possible. No matter what the age, no matter how carefully hidden, there exists the childlike part that considers life to be an adventure. Still there.

The Mind creates reality

A few weeks after the tragic rally of white nationalist and supremacists at the University of Virginia in Charlottesville resulted in the death and injury of some of the counter protestors, I had occasion to teach about the mind and how thoughts create our reality. It was a dynamic teaching event. I had prepared a talk to engage the group when, during the check-in (where each person gets to say a few words about themselves or answer a specific question), someone revealed an experience they'd had in Charlottesville, Virginia some time ago. The very mention of the place caused a visible reaction in the participants. My ability to be in the moment with the experience in the room rather than my carefully planned presentation helped unfold a powerful demonstration of the power of the mind. The teaching was each member of the *sangha*'s revelation of what the mind did in reaction to the name "Charlottesville," from the story created, to the body's reactions to the thoughts, the emotions that arose, the projections of thoughts and emotions to other participants, there was a cornucopia of responses to that word.

They were a demonstration of realities being created, and interacting with one another. And they—we, because I was engaged in it as well—had the experience of mind as creator. Suffering showed up in the room with some of the thoughts and the *sangha* saw how we create suffering with a thought. It was a direct, in-the-moment *experience* of the creation of suffering. I couldn't have choreographed what occurred. What I could do was be present to the teaching showing up in the room moment by moment. I may have had the intention to explore the mind with an idea of what it would look like, but what unfolded in the room was beyond expectation. A demonstration of the power of present moment awareness.

The City

I love being a city girl. One of the best parts is the excitement I feel when I see the New York City skyline, whether returning from a vacation trip or a silent meditation retreat. It's my unfailing response, but I also love meditation retreats that offer the opportunity to be in nature, to walk on the earth that responds to my every step where I make an impression. My retreat center is on beautiful forested land with creatures large and small and bodies of water to sit beside. In nature, it is easier to slow down and breathe deeply, to discard concerns, planning, and to-do lists—an opportunity to be merely in a body in space and time and to peer beneath the cloak of self that I've created.

At my first long retreat, I realized that the prior years of meditation and short retreats, as meaningful as they were, barely touched the surface of what's available in the exploration of both this body/mind/spirit and the world around me. The Seeing is sharper; the Hearing is amplified. I know myself and experience a renewed connection to the whole and what it is to be human that remains even when I return to the canyons of concrete glass and metal. The retreat space is like a clear body of water into which the me who arrives can immerse to uncover the one who knows, who remembers, enabling me to go home and live life from that space.

I sometimes have sitting meditations that are exquisite. Like a textbook version of what it can be like, if there is such a thing. And there are still days I sit with a mind on a road trip, where I wake up and look for the off-ramp to the present every two minutes. I sit with what comes— sensation in the body, a thought that arises. And when I awaken to being lost in thoughts of the past or future, I gently tell myself, "Okay. Come back to breathing in, then out, and return to awareness of the moment." Alive, aware, awake.

DHARMA AS CIVIL RIGHTS AND COMMUNITY TRANSFORMATION– ATLANTA STYLE

by Pamela Ayo Yetunde, ThD

While Jesus was dining at Levi's house, many tax collectors and sinners were eating with Him and His disciples—for there were many who followed Him.

—MARK 2:15

I gave support to caste because it stands for restraint. But at present caste does not mean restraint, it means limitations. Restraint is glorious and helps to achieve freedom. But limitation is like chain. It binds. There is nothing commendable in castes as they exist to-day. They are contrary to the tenets of the Shastras.

—MOHANDAS K. GANDHI

I am a Quaker. And as everyone knows, Quakers, for 300 years, have, on conscientious ground, been against participating in war. I was sentenced to three years in federal prison because I could not religiously and conscientiously accept killing my fellow man.

—BAYARD RUSTIN

Listen to the long stillness:
New life is stirring
New dreams are on the wing
New hopes are being readied:
Humankind is fashioning a new heart
Humankind is forging a new mind
God is at work.
This is the season of Promise.

—HOWARD THURMAN

We're living under the illusion that we have the power to determine
what to do with it.

—MORDECAI WYATT JOHNSON

In a real sense, all life is inter-related. All men are caught in an inescap-
able network of mutuality, tied in a single garment of destiny. Whatever
affects one directly, affects all indirectly. I can never be what I ought to
be until you are what you ought to be, and you can never be what you
ought to be until I am what I ought to be. . . . This is the inter-related
structure of reality.

—REV. DR. MARTIN LUTHER KING JR.

Meditation as a regular practice can allow one to better understand how things are connected to one another and dependent upon one another. For example, the Book of Mark, Gandhi, Rustin, Thurman, and Johnson all had an impact on King's embrace of Gandhi's *Satyagraha* or "truth force" to transform Atlanta and the US, from a viciously-enforced racially segregated city and country, to places where racial segregation is largely created by personal choice and economics. But when you think about Atlanta, you may think of King without thinking of his influencers.

When you hear the word "Atlanta," you may think of the King Center for Non-Violent Social Change; or "Hotlanta" due to the miserable mixture of heat and humidity during the summer; or "The ATL," a way of appreciating the hip cultures of the city; or the maddening traffic on the Spaghetti Junction of I-285 and I-85; or the lip-smacking fattening fried (sometimes double fried) southern cuisine. When you hear the word "Atlanta," you may feel gratitude for all the black people here as actor Danny Glover put it when he accepted the 2017 Golden Globe award for his show "Atlanta"; or you may think of Atlanta as the home of the Southern Christian Leadership Conference (SCLC) and the Black Civil Rights Movement of the 1960s. When you think of Atlanta, you may think of the historically black colleges and universities like Atlanta Clark, The Interdenominational Theological Center (ITC), Morehouse, and Spelman. You may also think of Georgia Tech, Emory, Mercer, and Georgia State. Historians may recall that W. E. B. DuBois taught at Atlanta University and wrote about Atlanta in *The Souls of Black Folks*. Rep. John Lewis and former United Nations Ambassador Andrew Young may also come to mind. You may think of Atlanta as the politically progressive city in the Bible Belt.

Many things come to mind when thinking about Atlanta, but you've probably never heard anyone say, "Oh, Atlanta, the city where people meditate!" But Atlantans meditate, and meditators have had a nearly invisible impact on the radical transformation of Atlanta's segregationist past. What transpired in Atlanta's spiritual implicate order was made manifest in Atlanta's material explicate order. The impact has been subtle yet powerful because King and the Civil Rights Movement adopted strategies that were influenced by Hindu meditators and Christian contemplatives—the kind of meditators and contemplatives who understand that we are all connected and that our existence is interdependent. Atlantans have been awakening to their interrelatedness for some decades and that awareness of our interrelatedness has resulted in a more livable, more humane, more civilized city. Ironically, our progress towards inclusivity is producing exclusive communities. The housing boom in Atlanta is deluding our interrelatedness, making Atlanta increasingly less affordable. To ebb the tide of economic exclusion, another word needs to be associated with Atlanta—meditate.

Many Atlantans meditate. Greater Atlanta is the ninth largest metropolitan area in the US with over 5,500,000 residents. Atlanta has professional sports teams, bars, high-rises, and densely populated neighborhoods. It has hosted the Olympic Games and it is home to the world's busiest airport. It has pollution and crime, but it has a southern friendliness you don't find in many other major cities. Perhaps the trees throughout the city make the difference. Within this large metropolitan area, amidst the hustle and bustle of cosmopolitan southern city life, Atlantans are meditating in many traditions.

Mindfulness practitioners, *vipassana* practitioners, yoga practitioners, and tantra meditators are keeping Atlanta open to lifestyles that are alternative to conventional urban busyness. These meditative forms, and their adherents, are supported in the greater Atlanta area by mindfulness groups like Breathing Heart *Sangha*; *vipassana* groups like Atlanta Insight Meditation Community, Sandy Springs Insight Meditation, and Roswell Insight Meditation; and *tantra* meditation supported by Drepung Loseling Monastery and Shambhala Meditation Center. Atlanta Soto Zen Center and Red Clay *Sangha* support meditation and meditation retreats in the Zen traditions. Dharma Jewel Monastery is a community supporting meditation in the

Taiwanese Chan Buddhist tradition. Soka Gakkai, in the Japanese Nichiren tradition, supports chanting and meditation. In the Hindu tradition, you will find Kashi Atlanta Urban Yoga Ashram. Interfaith communities like Vedanta Center support meditation, as do New Thought religious communities like Hillside International Truth Center. Ignatius House in Sandy Springs and Monastery of the Holy Spirit in Conyers are two Atlanta area Catholic communities that offer meditation retreats. There are many meditation and contemplative communities, in many religious and secular traditions, throughout greater Atlanta. Atlanta is a city that meditates.

Could Atlanta's rich history in community spiritual formation, along with its interfaith milieu and meditation communities, explain why it is also the second largest city to become a signatory to the Charter for Compassion? Atlanta is a city that is compassionate. With all this spiritual history and goodwill, how will Atlanta, the compassionate city that meditates, ebb the tide of costly housing in Atlanta?

I decided to visit the Mohandas Gandhi statue in Atlanta's Old Fourth Ward neighborhood, where King's childhood home and Ebenezer Baptist Church, where he preached, are located.

It may seem strange that I thought to visit the Gandhi statue about Atlanta's meditation culture and widening economic gap, but Gandhi has been a spirit guide for me for some time. I raised my daughter on the feature film about his life, I have a small portrait of him on my bookshelf, and I've asked for his guidance in the past. As a Buddhist practitioner who has practiced meditation almost daily since October 8, 2001, first through mindfulness, then through *vipassana*, then a bit through *tantra*, my intention was to engage in all three forms of meditation while standing before Gandhi's statue—a representation to me of compassion, courage, simplicity, humility, truthfulness, socio-economic-political action, and radical community transformation.

In *tantra* meditation, one puts before them a figure or image to visualize and incorporate the saint's attributes into one's self. It is said that St. Francis did the same thing with his image of Jesus on the cross. I believed if I practiced *tantra* meditation in front of Gandhi, I could possibly be inspired by Gandhi and King. On the heels of Donald J. Trump's presidential inauguration, I needed the compassion, courage, simplicity, humility, and truthfulness socio-economic-political activist spirit Gandhi could give me, if I am to contribute to an economic slowdown in a city that is driving out many Atlantans of color. As I meditated, here's what Gandhi told me.

Since we are connected, stay connected

The statue of Gandhi, an Indian Hindu, stands in close proximity to Ebenezer Baptist Church, the church of Dr. King Jr. and his father, Rev. King Sr., in a black community, in the Bible Belt. As an interfaith Buddhist practitioner, I understood Gandhi's presence in me to mean that when it comes to the power of meditation to transform societies like apartheid South Africa, British-occupied India, and segregated Atlanta, many Atlantans can continue to transform our city through the spiritual practices we are already engaging in.

Since we are connected, staying connected means expanding our interfaith dialogues

It may be the case that many Atlantans do not know that King, a Christian, took one of his greatest inspirations for transforming a racially-segregated country from Gandhi, a Hindu, who prayed and meditated in the *Bhagavad Gita Kriya* yoga tradition. King said that, although he had already heard about Gandhi, he immersed himself in books about Gandhi's movement after he heard Mordecai Wyatt Johnson, president of Howard

University, give a speech on his trip to India. It is said that King then engaged in interfaith dialogue by visiting Hindus and Gandhi followers in India, and reading the *Bhagavad Gita*. In the *Gita* (Stephen Mitchell's translation) it is written in Chapter 6, The Yoga of Meditation:

> *He who performs his duty*
> *with no concern for results*
> *is the true man of yoga—not*
> *he who refrains from action . . .*
> *. . . you first renounce your own selfish will.*
> *When a man has become unattached*
> *to sense-objects or to actions,*
> *renouncing his own selfish will,*
> *then he is mature in yoga . . .*
> *The man of yoga should practice*
> *concentration, alone,*
> *mastering mind and body,*
> *free of possessions and desires . . .*
> *he should concentrate, with his whole*
> *mind, on a single object;*
> *if he practices this way,*
> *his mind will soon become pure . . .*
> *When his mind has become serene*
> *by the practice of meditation,*
> *he sees the Self through the self*
> *and rests in the Self, rejoicing . . .*

King, from a Christian contemplative-Hindu meditation interfaith perspective, was a Christian and a man of yoga. It is important to note that the word "self" is spelled with a lower case "s" and an upper case "S" to denote the difference between one's body and mind—the lower case "s"—and universal consciousness/God—the upper case "S." And they merge through selfless meditation. Reading this passage from the *Gita* makes me think about King's "I've Been to the Mountain Top" speech where he said

> . . . *I just want to do God's will. And He's allowed me to go up to the mountain. And I've looked over. And I've seen the Promised Land . . . And so I'm happy, tonight. I'm not worried about anything. I'm not fearing any man! Mine eyes have seen the glory of the coming of the Lord!*

In this same speech, King talked about nonviolent (*ahimsa*) protesters having engaged in "transphysics," being [spiritual] masters in nonviolent protest, and cultivating a "dangerous unselfishness." Spiritual mastery, transphysics, and dangerous selfishness are all elements of Gandhi's *satyagraha*, informed by his understanding of the *Bhagavad Gita* integrated into his consciousness through meditation, and shared among King and his advisors.

Thurman met Gandhi and Thurman was King's spiritual advisor. Johnson went to India to learn about Gandhi's movement and returned to the US to give a speech about the movement, inspiring King to read about the movement. Rustin heard about Gandhi, then traveled to India and back to share those political strategies with King. And King went to India himself to learn how Gandhi and his followers transformed their country. Expanding our interfaith dialogues is necessary for the cultivation of civilization.

In Atlanta, there are several interfaith dialogue groups including Faith Alliance of Metro Atlanta, Interfaith Community Initiatives, Neshama

Interfaith Center, World Pilgrims, and the television network Atlanta Interfaith Broadcasters.

Become dangerously selfless through meditation

The *Bhagavad Gita* talks of a selflessness that arises through meditation. In the Insight Meditation Community (there are a few small Insight communities in Atlanta), our *vipassana* meditation is combined with a dangerous selfless ethos we call *brahmaviharas*, or Heavenly Abodes. This ethos includes compassion, lovingkindness, equanimity, and sympathetic joy. When practiced regularly over time, one is likely to experience the kind of selflessness that sees others' pain, accompanies that pain, thinks creatively about soothing the pain, and experiences joy for others' well-being. Dangerous selflessness, as it relates to the housing explosion in Atlanta, may require an economically subversive tactic.

Engage in economic withdrawal from a housing market that creates unaffordable housing

An idea worthy of exploration is for lower- and middle-income people to be willing to pool their monies to buy land collectively and build houses and apartments on it.

To be "still, in the city" of Atlanta is nothing new. Meditation and contemplation have been part of Atlanta's implicate fabric for about fifty years, alongside its higher education institutions, southern culture, intellectuals, dignitaries, theologians, black people, Civil Rights activists, airport, and the heat! Its many meditation and contemplation communities continue to hold space for the reality of our interconnectedness while supporting the city's interfaith dialogue engagements that support our aspirations toward being a compassionate city. The transformation in Atlanta over the last fifty years, thanks in large part to our lineage of public contemplative theologians like Johnson, Rustin, Thurman, and King, has been so tremendous that the Olympic Games were held here. The Olympics spawned another transformation—from a big city in the South to a metropolis in the country.

In the midst of population growth and the skyscraper transformation of our skyline, Gandhi's statue and the King Center for Nonviolent Social Change remain "low to the ground" and accessible to the people in the Old Fourth Ward, as reminders of the fact that oppressed people the world over have liberated themselves, and that oppressed people can continue to liberate ourselves. For all the great things Atlanta has become, we are forgetting our interconnectedness and it is manifesting in a new racial segregation based on economics. The spirits of Gandhi and King told me that to slow Atlanta's gentrification, we Atlantans need to: stay connected, expand our interfaith dialogues, become dangerously selfless through meditation, and engage in economic withdrawal from the housing market as it is now, to redirect those resources to alternative housing options. When we do these things, and do them well, people hearing "Atlanta" will think "Compassionate."

SANGHA AS THE WHOLE OF PRACTICE

by Tuere Sala

In October 2001, a dear friend pleaded with me to accompany her to a six-week beginning meditation class. I agreed to go but in no way thought of myself as a beginner! I had been practicing meditation on my own for over ten years; that year, however, had been particularly unsettling and the effectiveness of my practice was fading fast.

I had moved back home to Seattle in the summer of 1999. I left a ten-year career as a prosecuting attorney in Kansas City, Missouri. I was so happy to be going home and expected that I would just pick up where I left off. Life had a different plan. After initially failing the Washington Bar Exam, I took a job as a receptionist/administrative assistant until I got word in the fall of 2000 that I finally passed. The year 2001 brought with it a new job, a major earthquake in Seattle, the Bush administration, and 9/11. This beginning class came up just as I was losing my ability to keep the deep sense of uneasiness, panic, and growing rage contained within me.

My friend, who is white, and I arrived about twenty minutes early. I am a black woman and am used to being the only person of color in a room, but as the room steadily filled with white people and I remained the only person of color, I became increasingly troubled. The teacher was a white man whom I did not trust to be the best spiritual guide for an African American woman. It troubled me that he was teaching an Asian practice, that we had to take off our shoes, and that the two hours would be spent in silence. I spent the whole twenty minutes before class sitting there arguing with myself; my head swimming in a sea of fearmongering, complaining, and judgment. I kept feeling the impulse to get up and leave. I would whisper to my friend, "I'm leaving" or "I don't want to be here" or "I know this is going to be stupid" or "I shouldn't be here." My friend just kept whispering back, "Please, for me?" or "I need you, please stay," or "Just stay with me tonight and you don't have to come back." We agreed I would stay that night but she was on her own for the rest of the class series.

Nothing in life seems truly random to me anymore and that class was no exception. What I heard that night would have a profound effect on the rest of my life. The teacher talked about practice as a guide to move through the world rather than a tool to make oneself better. Time and time again, he reiterated that there was nothing we needed to fix and if we were willing to pay attention we could see our way out of any difficulty. Throughout the evening, I kept feeling a sense of deep hopefulness. His words allowed everything I had read and practiced over the last ten years to come alive. The teacher would ultimately support me in untangling myself from deeply held childhood fear, in pulling back the veil of anger to reveal its emptiness, and in finding my way to genuine joy. Seattle Insight, the organization that offered the class, would become my home, my place of refuge, my *sangha*.

Sangha is a Pali word representing the community of practitioners of Buddha's teachings. It is one of the three refuges—Buddha, *dharma*, and *sangha*. The three refuges represent the foundation of a practitioner's strength and encouragement. We find this strength and encouragement in the life of the historical Buddha and his efforts to awaken, in the light and wisdom of the *dharma*, and from the support of the *sangha*. So much has been written and spoken of around Buddha and the *dharma* that we sometimes forget the importance of *sangha*. For Buddha, however, *sangha* was everything.

There is a famous story where Ananda, Buddha's foremost student, said to the Buddha that *"Sangha,* with its friendship, its companionship, and its camaraderie, is half of the holy life." Buddha's reply was *"No! The sangha, with its friendship, its companionship, and its camaraderie, is the whole of the holy life."* Seattle Insight helped me understand Buddha's proclamation to Ananda: *sangha*, with its relational twists and turns, is the whole of practice.

The way Buddha set up his initial *sangha* is so inspiring to me. He enjoined monastics with lay people, creating a world where the two were fully dependent upon each other. Monastics depended upon the lay community for their life necessities, and the lay community depended upon the monastics for guidance, encouragement, and support in life's transitions. Both groups followed Buddha's Eightfold Path of an awakened life, although in very different ways, as monastic and householder, and yet they also followed the path together as *sangha*. It was their shared intention towards renunciation, goodwill, and harmlessness that sustained their continued journey on the path and why we still follow this path more than 2500 years later.

Over the course of fifteen years of practicing at Seattle Insight, I participated in this shared intention and learned the meaning of lovingkindness, of courage, of compassion, and of the nature of a balanced warrior's spirit. I began teaching at Seattle Insight several years ago and am currently a co-guiding teacher. This chapter is my humble offering to my beloved *sangha*.

Historical perspective

No one was with me when I set out on my commitment to follow the Eightfold Path. It began in the spring of 1991 with a crisis of faith—a kind of religious breakdown, if you will. I had graduated from law school but failed the Kansas bar and then had to quit the job I begged God to give me because it was contingent on me passing the bar. I then spent another year studying and taking the Missouri Bar, which I had just received notice I had failed. I was a single mother of two boys and basically was realizing I was going to remain unemployed and had no idea what to do. I was broke, two months behind on my rent, dodging every collection agency in the State of Missouri, and I'm pretty sure my therapist was ready to cut me loose for spotty payments. I figured God must have hated me or at least was, yet again, very disappointed in the mess I had made of my life.

The crisis hit me as I was getting ready for church, just as I did most every Sunday. I was feeling tired and weary trying to fix my hair. The longer I stood before the mirror, the more I could see the weariness on my face and body. I looked so beaten down to myself that it was hard for me to look at myself. I tried to look only at my hair, but no matter what I did to my hair I could not hide my face from myself. The longer I fussed with my hair the madder I got. This surge of rage rose up from the bottom of my feet and throughout my entire body. I was so pissed! I stood there having what can only be described as a negative "aha" moment, realizing I had fallen for the scam. I had been hoodwinked, conned, taken in by the adults in my childhood who swore about the benefits of hard work and perseverance. I was pissed at my parents, the church, and God.

I had just spent the bulk of my adult life in college and law school or preparing for them. I had scratched out a living on welfare and low-wage jobs. I rarely had enough money to sustain even my basic living expenses and would spend hours on the phone pleading with the electric company, the gas company, or the phone company to restore my service or give me a little more time before turning off the service. I put in long hours studying, washing clothes, cooking, cleaning, and grocery shopping. I took care of my boys, doing everything I could to keep their spirits high, though I was rarely able to do anything special for them. I had foregone so many things because of what I thought getting a law degree would bring.

"As soon as I get through with this semester; as soon as I get this internship; as soon as I get my degree; as soon as I get this student loan, that job, pass this class, that exam . . . things will be better." This was my constant mantra to myself and to my boys. Just hold on a little longer and things would be much better in the future. Now I was standing in the bathroom looking in the mirror at living proof that things were not better, and for the first time that I could remember, I didn't believe that the future would get any better. I sat down on the toilet lid and cried. I remember this cry because I was not crying about my circumstances, I was crying about no longer having an illusion I could hold on to. I was lost.

I sat there doubting everything. I doubted whether getting an education really made a difference. I doubted whether it was right for me to put the boys through such a difficult life. I doubted whether paying money for therapy would ever "fix" me. I began to think that maybe I had been fooling myself all this time. I even began to doubt the existence of God, thinking maybe this religious thing really was designed by the rich and powerful to keep the masses down. Everything I believed in was giving way under my feet as if the very foundation of my life was being washed away in the rushing floodwaters. I went to church that Sunday and nearly every Sunday after, but it was not the same. I had lost something, something I needed in order to keep living the lonely, overworked, forever-searching life I had carved out for myself. I had lost the illusion of the "better tomorrow."

What happened to me that Sunday was recognition of the three characteristics of human existence—impermanence, dissatisfaction, and emptiness. Everything about human existence is impermanent because we live in a world based upon unstable conditions that are always subject to change. This instability cannot be controlled, making all of our efforts to control life ultimately unsatisfactory. Moreover, everything in life is without inherent substance, aside from the significance, identity, and meaning we give it. I thought putting my attention and trust in accomplishment would bring me closer to something better. I thought the only thing I had going for me was the future. I believed that if I could control the future, I could make my life and myself better. Until it hit me that I was living the same story over and over again—different cities, different apartments, different relationships, but the same story. I could no longer trick myself into believing something better was coming. I came face to face with an enormous question; if life was nothing more than a series of bad events, how would I ever be truly happy?

To get an answer, I went to the only place I ever went to find answers to questions—the book store. I walked up and down the aisles looking for information. I read from books in the philosophy section. I read from books in the psychology section. I read from the self-help books. But nothing seemed to answer my questions. I didn't need to learn about why I was having bad times, how to deal with them, or how to heal from bad times; that was nothing more than the same thing I had been learning my whole life.

I had books to help me understand my childhood sexual abuse, books to help me get over the abuse, and books to help me live with it. I had been in therapy ten years working on the abuse. I had books on affirmations, journaling, and daily reminders. I had materials from seminars, classes, and weekend workshops. I had had enough of trying to get away from bad times and the sexual abuse. I had come to accept that my life would always be full of bad times because of my abuse. I wanted to learn how to be genuinely happy in such a life.

Then I stumbled upon *Training the Mind and Cultivating Loving-Kindness* by Chogyam Trungpa, a book that ultimately answered my questions and turned my life in a different direction. Over the next ten years, I read that book cover to cover, over and over. Whenever I got to the end I would simply start over at the beginning. I still have and use the original book. It was my gateway to the *dharma*.

The book taught me to look into the depths of my habitual tendencies to find happiness. I associated habits with things you do like smoking or drinking. I never considered ways of being as habitual. I learned to see my habits in everything: how I put my shoes on, how I sat in the car, what I chose to eat, and whom I chose to hang out with. In looking at all these habits I could also see how many things I needed to go my way in order to be happy, and the impossibility of it all. I recognized that if everything about me was habitual, then everything about everyone else was habitual. All this habitual energy left us impulsively reacting and overreacting to everything. It slowly began to occur to me that suffering was in this habitual, uncontrollable reactivity, and happiness lay in the non-reactivity. It was in my resistance to the impulse of my habits that I would abide in happiness. I believed meditation was the practice that would teach me how to resist. I bought more books.

I read several books about how to meditate. I didn't have a teacher, so I taught myself what I thought was meditation. I simply practiced whatever I read. In the beginning, however, I had three problems. I was black, Christian, and lived in Kansas City, Missouri—not exactly the Buddhist capital of the country. I didn't know anything about being part of a community of practitioners like a *sangha*; and the couple of times I mentioned at church that I was trying to learn how to meditate, it didn't go over too well. Frankly, I was a little scared of the practice myself. The only thing I knew about meditation was what I had seen on TV or read in a book back in the mid-1970s. I didn't even know there were others like me who practiced. I wasn't completely convinced that it wasn't some form of devil-worshipping and feared my practice might somehow harm my boys. So, I practiced in secret—mostly in a closet in my apartment.

My practice consisted of simply sitting quietly and either counting my breaths or reading. I thought the whole idea of meditation was to not think. I would sit quietly telling myself the whole time to stop thinking. What I was looking for in these early years was peace of mind or rather a respite from the weariness. I was going through a lot in therapy and my practice kept me from jumping off a bridge or going to jail for killing somebody. I would be gentle to myself; giving myself lovingkindness or compassion.

Looking back, I can see I was just sitting and daydreaming happy thoughts and enjoying the peaceful state of mind I was in. If anything unpleasant came up, I would try to ignore it and get back to my peaceful state. If, for some reason, I could not get peaceful, I would get up and try again later. I found a sense of ease and calmness but I wasn't present to anything. As far as I was concerned, this was meditation.

In the summer of 1991, I took and passed the Missouri bar exam on the second try. I worked as a prosecuting attorney with the City of Kansas City, Missouri, and later with the Jackson County Prosecutor's Office. For the next ten years, my life was consumed with the practice of law, understanding the Eightfold Path, and meditation.

Practitioner's perspective

I was committed to my meditation practice, but it was limited. I didn't have the capacity to face alone deeply destructive habits of mind. I didn't understand how to relax, observe, and allow discomfort. I could force myself to be patient with an uncomfortable situation, but it didn't make sense to simply be with it and not do anything to fix the problem that was making the situation uncomfortable. My best efforts would fade and I would often lose momentum. I was sincere about practice and at the same time could be easily distracted and restless.

As a practical matter, an intention of renunciation, goodwill, and harmlessness is a bit contrary to the habitual nature of human existence. As humans, we are steeped in the underlying tendencies towards greed, hatred, and delusion. These tendencies are hardwired within our DNA and create a tremendous energy current when we encounter the larger world. We are besieged at every turn with advertisements proclaiming the need for comfort through the accumulation of things. Simultaneously, the world with all its abundance ignores, or barely cares about, the suffering of others. The media and social networks inundate us with disconnected stories of the anguish and grief of others, stories used to make money, for political gain, to generate a following. We can easily become swept away in passion and anger with the realities of excess, waste, social injustice, apathy, and the blatant cruelty of mankind.

When I practiced alone, I found it easier to simply shut down from this added pain in my life. I could sit quietly and my practice would bring me peacefulness. I could remember my commitment and re-center myself. My commitment to renunciation, goodwill, and harmlessness, which was tremendous in my life, seemed so small in the context of the larger world.

The first night at that Seattle Insight beginning class I realized I needed to be with others who were also trying to be with discomfort who were just as committed to renunciation, goodwill, and harmlessness as I was. I needed the stillness of others to remind me how to connect with my own stillness. I needed the guidepost of a regular *sangha* to keep me on the path.

I realized that night that I could seriously liberate the mind in this lifetime. I could let go and simply look at the reality of experience without needing to change or fix it. Thus began my gradual shift into *sangha*.

Seattle Insight is one of the largest *sanghas* in the country. In 2001, it was 99.99 percent white with one African American—me (although it is still primarily white, there are considerably more people of color attending). We met weekly for two hours consisting of a forty-minute meditation, forty-five-minute *dharma* teaching, and a question/answer period. The entire two hours was in silence except for questions to the teacher. I spoke to no one and no one spoke to me. There were some practitioners who knew each other and spoke quietly to each other, as I did with my friend whenever she would come to the sit. Mostly, however, we did our talking in the car or outside before or after the sit.

The beginning instructions for the foundations of a formal mindfulness practice are to start with concentrating on the breath, then move inward towards noticing the feeling tones of pleasant, unpleasant, or neutral and then open to thoughts and emotions. With the breath as the focal point, you sit quietly and watch the rising and falling of things like sound, sensations, feeling tones, thoughts, and/or emotions. I found myself unable to do this, even though I thought I had been practicing for many years. I knew I was breathing, but I couldn't feel it. I thought the only feeling tone I had was neutral as I could not sense pleasant or unpleasant as a feeling tone. And rarely was I able to tell when I was thinking or having an emotion of any kind. For some reason, I could not experience anything and now my once-peaceful sitting practice had somehow turned into nothing more than a boring "waiting" practice filled with intermittent periods of sleepiness and restlessness.

Week after week I kept showing up. To be honest, I can't say exactly why. I just felt pulled to this group. All I know is that the ability to sit quietly in a low-lighted room and listen to the teachings of the Buddha was the most compelling period of my week. The energy was so powerful some evenings that I could barely leave. There was a sense that I could take on anything, and that, together, we were bigger than the complacency and cruelty of the world. My shared intentions of renunciation, goodwill, and harmlessness were no longer lofty wishes. They were real possibilities in any given moment. I felt as though I had the power to change the world.

I assumed if I could figure out the ultimate goal of meditation, I would be able to master it. The concept itself made sense to me. In order to experience peace, we must see what is holding us from it. Sitting quietly, without judgment, allows us to see what is holding us back. With that in mind, week after week, I gathered my courage and went, and, believe me, it took courage to walk into a large room as the only black person amongst nearly two hundred white people so I could learn about a subject that didn't make any sense. But I kept showing up because every week I thought this was going to be the night I would relax into peace.

It is not easy for black people to feel safe in all-white environments. I am not talking about safety in terms of physical harm, I am speaking about being safe enough to be yourself and have a sense that you are included in the group. Now I have been attending this same group for over fifteen years, and feel very connected and loved, but in the beginning, I felt a palpable unease from the way people related to my presence there, as if at any minute someone was going to ask me to leave. It seemed I would walk into the room with stares, take a seat with stares, and watch people walk by staring at me. It was as if I heard, "What are you doing here?" or "How did you get in here?" It was rough at times, but I could not bring myself to leave my teacher. I started going to the weekly sits because of him and had a strong sense that he was going to be a powerful influence on me. I just kept showing up even with the staring and my own restlessness and sleepiness.

Eventually someone told me about a small practitioners of color (POC) meditation group, and I began practicing with both groups, getting instruction from my teacher with the large group and trying out the instructions during the smaller POC group. Most of the POCs I knew in Seattle hated attending Seattle Insight because of the isolation and silence. Many saw it as creating a lack of community and social engagement. But for someone who had spent ten years of practice in solitude, this worked fine for me. I was just attending for the teachings. I wasn't looking for friendship, companionship, or camaraderie. I was just looking for an awakened mind, which seemed like a private, personal thing to me. I was quite content to not have to "smile and be nice."

Citta is the Pali word for heartmind and it refers to the knowing quality of the heart. One of my closest teachers is Venerable Dr. Pannavati, founder of Heartwood Refuge Retreat Center. She and I were talking about the nature of *sangha* when she shared with me that heartmind also represented *sangha*. She said that when we attend a center to hear the *dharma* and go home—there is wisdom but no heart. We need the interaction with other people to open the heart and that is heartmind—that is *sangha*.

I found myself wanting to be of service to others in whatever capacity I could find. Seattle Insight rented space from various churches. Volunteers were needed to set up and take down the room every week. Quite out of the blue, I found myself raising my hand to sign up as a volunteer to set up and take down the sound system. I couldn't believe I had agreed to do this, given that I was completely lost around electronics. I started volunteering for lots of things and the more I volunteered the more I got to know people and more people got to know me.

Sangha's perspective

Which brings me to the final aspect of *sangha*. Greg Kramer, a teacher and founder of the relational meditative practice of Insight Dialogue, once told me that *sangha* was *dharma* plus love. I think this a beautiful phrase that captures *sangha* for what it truly can be in our lives. Spiritual friendship is at the heart of *sangha*. This spiritual friendship keeps us all strong and committed as we walk this path to awakening together. We sit with one another and at the same time we sit for one another. Together we can have the courage to move into the unknown, to abandon our habits of mind, and to step into our Buddha nature. We can experience both the relative and ultimate realities of practice.

From the outside looking in, Buddhism and/or mindfulness appears to be an individual practice. Each of us meditates, studies, and contemplates the *dharma* individually, leaving us to mistakenly believe that liberation of the mind is personal. True investigation, however, arises in relationship. We need the tension, discomfort, laughter, and passion that come from "relationship with" to experience the depth of freedom. This tension is often thought of as the shadow side of *sangha,* but in many respects, it is the liberating side of *sangha*.

I'm not sure of the exact time, but sometime around 2005, Seattle Insight began alternating between what we called Talk nights and Discussion nights. Discussion nights created opportunities for us to share our thoughts, impressions, and feelings about practice. Being a POC in a room full of white people became more of a problem for me when we started having open discussion nights. I didn't feel safe enough to speak freely about my experiences.

Many good-natured white people have a habit of assuming life's circumstances should be the same for anyone as it is for them. I don't always understand why this is so, given the amount of diversity in this country.

Maybe we as POCs should be more outspoken about our differences and/or maybe white people should pay more attention to what POCs actually say. In any event, I found it particularly uncomfortable to sit in small intimate circles and talk to strangers about the challenges in my life.

I learned something, however, from those small intimate circles. I learned practice is practice no matter what race or nationality we may be. We are all entangled with a comparing mind, with a mind inclining towards defining who or what is inferior, superior, and equal. I watched as my mind constantly watched and evaluated what others did in comparison to me. I found that when I used whatever difficulty or challenge that presented itself in one of those circles as an opportunity for practice, I could see how much we are all trying to measure up against another. I could see how easily a state of mind like pride, boastfulness, jealousy, envy, and intolerance can show up. It's not that any one of us sets out to be jealous or intolerant of another person. It arises out of our habitual nature—our non-awareness of underlying tendencies. I learned to see that much of our problem comes from the mind—not reality.

I believe this complexity is a necessary part of the strength of *sangha*. It is what makes us different from a social group. The kind of spiritual friendship that Buddha was pointing towards is not there to simply lull us into complacency. *Sangha* is about being in *dharma* friendship, not social friendship. Often our social friendships don't go deep enough for awakening. *Dharma* friendships live in the world of difficulty. The very nature of this kind of friendship is meant to rub up against us, to bring out our tendencies towards greed, hatred, and delusion, and to shine a light on our habits of mind. We are, without a doubt, relational beings. We need relationship to survive. We also need relationship for liberation.

By 2006, I was living in extremes—extreme anxiety, extreme anger, and extreme sadness. I had the sense this was all coming up because of my practice. I was torn between wanting to stop the whole thing and wanting to persevere to the end—if for no other reason than to see if Buddha's proclamation that ending suffering was possible. For a good five years, I couldn't practice alone. I had no daily practice. I had to sit with others, and even then, I was barely able to sit still.

As difficult as this period was, I believe it was necessary for real freedom and genuine happiness. I believed life to be some permanent and perpetual state of existence that I was forever striving to control, that whatever circumstances I was born into, my level of intelligence, my amount of education, money, and access to resources said something about who I was and how my life was supposed to be. I lived trying to acquire enough resources to limit life's impact upon me. If my life went along smoothly with fewer interruptions, irritations, and obstacles, I was happy. I basically put my trust in various crutches—job, health, freedom—to minimize the effects of the world upon me.

In truth, however, life is a series of moments unrelated to each other but for our stringing them together through reliance on the crutches. In any given moment one of these crutches could be stripped away, leaving us completely exposed and unprotected. Coming face to face with the ineffectiveness of the crutches in keeping us free from suffering can be quite unsettling. Looking back, I realize that no amount of work to better myself was going to bring me happiness if it didn't exist in the present moment.

Somehow over the years I built a sense of trust that I could practice with others. No one would care what it looked like. I just needed to be in the room, to practice in this moment. I let go of trying to get rid of the anxiety, the anger, and the sadness. I just wanted to be in a room with people I knew did not think it so crazy to want to take the time to investigate the nature of suffering. Slowly over time, my anxiety lessened, my anger cooled, and my sadness turned into the sweetest experience of compassion.

Meditating regularly at Seattle Insight, the POC group, and retreats, I noticed my practice was becoming deeper. I felt an inner capacity growing stronger within me. I believe this is what happens when we sit together with a community of practitioners. This shared intention of renunciation, goodwill, and harmlessness generates its own energetic current of stillness and inner capacity. I was tapping into what Buddha taught as lovingkindness and compassion.

Over the course of my years at Seattle Insight, I was rebuilding my inner core in a way I never could have done alone. Sitting in a room with two hundred people at varying levels of inner kindness and compassion created a vortex of lovingkindness. Unbeknownst to me, the kindness and care being generated from people I barely spoke a word to was having a tremendous effect on my life.

I experienced quite a bit over the fifteen years I spent practicing with Seattle Insight. Some of it was easy, like at a volunteer appreciation event when the host asked everyone who had volunteered over the previous year to please stand, and everyone in the room stood. Some of it was not so easy, as when the church we were using had an infestation of bedbugs and we had to quickly find a new location and move the *sangha* to it. There were times when I was filled with compassion listening to the pain of others, times I was brightened by the joy of sharing practice insights with good friends, and still times when I was consumed with anger, vowing never to return. Through it all, I let go of parts of myself I thought defined me and touched into parts of myself I never knew existed.

Teacher's perspective

The response that comes up most when I open to the experience of Seattle Insight is gratitude. Gratitude is made up of connection, appreciation, generosity, and forgiveness. Being a part of a *sangha* provides us the opportunity to serve others and express our generosity. Being a teacher provides me an opportunity to inspire a fellow practitioner. Together we diminish the influence of greed, hatred, and delusion and fill our practice with motivation, reassurance, and enthusiasm.

Zen Master Thich Nhat Hanh is known for saying that "It is possible that the next Buddha will not take the form of an individual. The next Buddha may take the form of a community, a community practicing understanding and lovingkindness, a community practicing mindful living." Think about this for a moment. The Buddha, an enlightened being, would be a group of people, not one person. This Buddha would be a completely different type of being than what I can currently conceive. Right now, when we think of a being we think of a single entity; a single consciousness. We think of Buddha this way—a single being.

But what if the next Buddha was a collective? Not in a "groupthink" way because that is a group of people with a single thought, which is basically a single being. What if Buddha represented "collective consciousness"? Consciousness that contained and accepted "all." What if the idea of a comparing mind was considered old school? Human beings somehow understood the wisdom and brilliance of diversity the way nature understands. What if we realized the truth inherent in the statement that "one cannot be free unless all are free"? I can conceive of awakening in this body based upon my own practice, but what if awakening were to occur within the body of *sangha*? There are thousands of *sanghas* around the world. Is it possibly the greatest potential for a great awakened world?

Although I can't fully conceive of how this would come into being, I can fully appreciate its implications. I spent over ten years teaching mindfulness and nonviolent communication to men and women in prisons surrounding the Seattle metropolitan area. Even as a prosecutor, I could find *sangha* within various prison walls. I also found ways to bring mindfulness to some of Seattle's most marginalized people. There is a way that we inspire each other when we share the *dharma*, and that inspiration has a rippling effect. It is in that rippling effect that collective consciousness abides and has its greatest potential.

In the fall of 2010, I started a two-year Community Dharma Leader training program through Spirit Rock Retreat Center. This was a significant turning point in my practice. It was as significant as the Sunday I realized there was nothing better coming my way; that first evening of the Seattle Insight beginning meditation class, and my final reconnection with my body. The significance of this training was that I realized that I wanted practice to take a center place in my life. I no longer wanted practice to be something I did after work. I wanted practice to be my life. In December 2013 I retired from the practice of law and chose instead to live off the generosity of others.

This was an enormous shift in my worldview. Over twenty-five years of practice, I had found a level of trust in the universal kindness in human beings; I had developed a sense of security even in unknown futures; and I had cultivated a deep joy in simplicity. I am truly happier today than I have ever been. I still live with the same difficulties I had when I started this path but without the sting of dread, depression, and overwhelm. I know how to connect to a genuine happiness regardless of the conditions that exist in my life.

In conclusion, I want to share a story told by someone just starting out in this practice. She began by saying she hoped we would comprehend this better than her family, but she would understand if it didn't make sense to us either. She shared that she, her husband, and her son went on a long trip away from home. Unbeknownst to them, something was left out or open that generated a lot of flies in the house. When they returned, in their urgent distress, they began to get rid of all the flies. She found herself being very conflicted about the killing of the flies. She shared this with her husband and son and asked if there was some other way to get rid of the flies without killing them. Her husband and son looked at her, looked at each other, and burst into laughter. They basically went back to the process of getting rid of the flies.

At some point later, she went to lie down on her bed. She was in the room alone with just her dog. Suddenly she heard a fly. Her body immediately reacted back to the earlier energy, until she realized no one was in the room but her. She lay there peacefully on the bed: her, her dog, and the fly. She shared that it was such a beautiful moment she could barely explain it. When she got up she tried to explain it to her family, but they just could not understand.

When she finished, I asked the room for a show of hands if they understood—everyone's hand went up.

PRACTICING IN PRISON CITY

by Ellen Furnari and Walt Opie

Ellen Furnari:

> *The best way to describe a prison is to think of it as a small city.*
> —WARDEN STEPHEN BULLARD,
> DONALDSON CORRECTIONAL FACILITY
> (QUOTE FROM 2008 DOCUMENTARY FILM
> *THE DHAMMA BROTHERS*)

I was surprised recently when I referred to the prison where I volunteer as a terrible city, where no one would choose to live. Almost immediately one of the Buddhist *sangha* members spoke up to contradict me. He said he felt sorry for those of us who live outside the prison, in other cities. We have so much to distract us, so much to be attached to, so many impediments to practice. Here in the prison city, he said, there is so little to be attached to—barely adequate food, few possessions, very little entertainment—so it is conducive to letting go, to focusing instead on meditation, almost like a Buddhist monastery. I felt rightly corrected. And once again moved by the depth of practice of many of our *sangha* members in prison.

It is easy to think of this California prison as a terrible city whose residents have been convicted of various crimes. Prisons are generally overcrowded, poorly constructed, noisy, providing almost no privacy, and with tremendous limitations on health care, education, and other activities. Prisons are an incredibly violent place to live. Prison workers are so poorly paid they have been compared to slaves. Staff members who come to work there would never wish to live there, nor want their families there. And in the prison where I am a volunteer Buddhist chaplain, most of the men were shaped by conditions in the cities where they grew up. Many were harmed by rampant racism, discrimination, poverty-stricken and stressed-out families, and poor education and health systems that characterize so many American cities.

The topic I was talking about this particular day comes from *Anguttara Nikaya*. I read these two translations:

All things are rooted in the will (born of desire). All things come to actual existence through attention. All things arise from contact. All things converge on feelings (pleasant, unpleasant or neither). Of all things, the foremost is concentration. All things are mastered by mindfulness. Of all things, the highest is wisdom. In all things, the essence is liberation . . .

and

Rooted in desire, friends, are all things. Born of attention are all things. Arisen from contact are all things. Converging on feeling are all things. Headed by concentration are all things. Dominated by mindfulness are all things. Surmountable by wisdom are all things. Yielding deliverance as essence are all things.

And I opened a discussion asking, if all things in essence yield deliverance, or liberation, or are of themselves liberation, then how does living in this prison city, in essence, yield deliverance, yield true freedom? I witness, over and over again, the truth of this, in the day-to-day practice of residents who have no access to retreats, to privacy, to quiet beautiful places to meditate, and who are living in a context where they have very little freedom in their day-to-day activities. And so, we reflected together on the strength of their practice, challenges, and opportunities.

What does it mean to practice in prison, with an intention, an inclination toward true freedom? For me as a *sangha* member and volunteer chaplain and for the residents of the city, every experience, every encounter, every thing, holds the potential to be a pathway to freedom, to being fully awake and knowing things as they actually are. Each holds, at essence, the capacity to be the vehicle for deliverance from the suffering we all live with, small and large. To say this in the midst of a prison was both scary and important.

Several men spoke to their own experience with this teaching. One talked about how he realized that this planet is just one planet among millions, it will eventually die, and new planets will be born, and that everything is being born and dying all the time. And how this helped him experience many things in prison, which used to be very challenging, as just more of the flow of things being born and dying, each experience impermanent. Another talked about how he tries to be mindful throughout his day, to what is going on, being in the actual experience, rather than his reactions, thoughts, etc.

Over the several years of sitting with these *sanghas*, we have explored basic Buddhist teachings and how we practice with them. The traditional teaching identifies three pillars of Buddhist practice—in Pali these are *dana, sila*, and *bhavana*. *Dana* is generosity, *sila* is ethical behavior or virtue, and *bhavana* is meditation or concentration. In our prison city *sanghas*, we study, practice, and reflect on all three.

Generosity. There are numerous ways to be generous. One form of generosity happens when we have all day (8:30–3:30) mini-retreats of silent practice together in one of the *sanghas*. Several of the residents share cooking ahead of time, and make a meal for all the residents who are participating. Because of prison rules, we outside *sangha* members can't share our food with residents, nor they with us. But this sharing, this generosity, is very meaningful. For one, it is a gift to others, a very welcome break from daily prison food. But even more, in the prison dining hall, residents for the most part sit segregated by race. So, this is one of the few times that residents of several races sit together and share a meal. And they report a strong sense of sharing and connection, even though it is all (or almost all) in silence.

A few *sangha* members strongly feel the presence of hungry ghosts (*pretas*) in their buildings. They regularly bring back a small amount of food from their meals to offer to the hungry ghosts along with water. We have talked about how there are literal hungry ghosts in other realms, and the humans who behave as hungry ghosts—never satisfied, poisoned by what they do take in, driven by craving that cannot be satisfied. And how living in very close proximity to people who suffer in this way (sharing a bunk bed) provides many challenges.

Other *sangha* members are generous with time, listening to each other, offering support and care to many of the people around them. Now and again a new person comes to Buddhist services and mentions they have come because one of our *sangha* has been so kind, supportive, and attentive to their struggles.

Ethical Behavior. We talk about *sila,* or ethical behavior, in many ways. To begin with, we review the precepts at most services: 1) I strive to practice not killing or harming other living beings; 2) I strive to practice taking only what is freely given; 3) I strive to practice responsible sexual conduct;

4) I strive to practice speaking truthfully; and 5) I strive to protect my mental health through mindful consumption and to avoid intoxicants. Periodically we spend time studying each one, particularly when there are a number of new members. Each time we study them, I learn something.

A common experience after coming to Buddhist services for a while is to notice and care about all life forms around the prison. Men talk about seeing a spider and taking it outside, so no one will step on it.

One *sangha* member struggled with himself for a long time about becoming a vegetarian. As he reflected on the precept of not taking life, he thought about the animals he was eating. But he didn't want to give up meat. For several months, he brought this up for discussion during discussion periods. In the end, I think he decided to keep eating meat, but to be aware of the animals he was eating as life forms. He was transferred to another prison shortly after, so I don't know if that settled with him or not.

I feel a deeper understanding of the precept of not taking what isn't given. In our society, which is built on stealing land, on slave labor, our childhoods have not been freely given to abusers; in anger, we have tried to take another person's sense of self-worth through our words; as well as being impeccable about only taking what has been offered and not stealing.

Another precept addresses right speech, and *sangha* members give examples of being very careful with their speech, not engaging so much in gossip, walking away from angry attacks rather than responding.

Concentration. For a number of months, we shared the chapel, where we meet every week to meditate together, with a Protestant group. One night we are sitting in the chapel with the divider down the middle, which is mostly a visual barrier rather than blocking sound. Born-again Christians testifying to Jesus are on the other side, loudly singing, clapping, and shouting. We are meditating. Can sound be just sound? Can we be with what arises—irritation, anger, and memories, and return to the breath, to awareness of the body? Afterwards, during check-in, someone talks about being abused by their minister, the feelings that arose during this meditation, and how he stayed with it, eventually reaching a place of more ease.

Another night, we could hear loud intense music from a film playing on the other side of the divider. But as we sit together, I have such a strong sense of quiet, in the space between sounds, peacefulness. During check-in, one man shares how he just concentrated on his breath. He meditates in other places daily, but when we sit together, it is so much more peaceful and quiet, and he really didn't notice the music very much.

During their day-to-day lives in the prison city, some men wake up very early to meditate when it is quiet. They meditate lying on their bunks, as they can't go anywhere else. Those on Level III live in cells with generally one bunk bed and two residents. Many of them find this a particularly good place to meditate. Some do yoga or Tai Chi in the early morning, mindfully, when they are allowed to move. Some find a relatively quiet place during the day, in a corner here or there. And some just figure it is noisy and chaotic and they just sit when and where they want. A few do walking meditation, walking around the yard, when they are allowed out.

Many report that when they meditate regularly, they are calmer. And when they don't get to it, they really notice. One man had been interested in Buddhism for a while, but never really practiced. During the several years he was in jail, as his case wound its way through the courts, he started to meditate. Having been given a long sentence means, at his age, he will die in prison. And he has been meditating in his cell for several hours a day. He says he feels less agitation and "upset-ness" about this turn in his life, more a sense of how it doesn't matter where you are and that there are opportunities to see into the emptiness of experience. And at the same time, he tutors other prison city residents who are studying for the GREs, shares his Buddhist books with others, encourages and supports other *sangha* members. So, his practice reveals both emptiness and kindness to others.

Fruits of practice. Some residents note that their practice has literally saved their lives. They have chosen to live peacefully and not harm others, which has meant walking away from fights, separating out from gangs and other previous associations. At his first time coming to Buddhist services, one resident shared, with tears coming down his face, that it was like coming in from the jungle to a peaceful sanctuary.

Another shared that recently he felt like someone had pushed his buttons, and he felt his old self rising up. He told the other resident "You don't know me" and was about to show him violently who he was. But then he took a breath and walked away. Starting a fight would have gotten him time in solitary as well as points against ever being released. At our check-in, after telling us this, he said this has been churning for several days. He had to come to services that night to find his peace again. With a big smile, he assured us he had found his peace, here, together, in the midst of the music and other noise, and the depths of our stillness together.

At the close of an all-day mini-retreat, we go around the circle, giving each person time to share, if he'd like. After his first time coming to the all-day, one resident noted that after twenty years in prison, this was the first time he had found quiet.

Ultimately though, we don't practice to "get" anything. One resident shared that during his trial and appeals, while in jail, he had practiced very hard—doing a lot of meditation, reading, and praying. When he lost his appeals and was sent to prison, he felt that Buddhism and other religions had let him down and didn't really work. He felt anger and despair, and was hugely upset. But then one day, he realized that he just needed to give himself to the practice, and not expect or want to "get" anything from it. From that time on, he has meditated and read and is a core member of our *sangha*, a very peaceful presence. I was blown away the day he shared this story, as it made me realize how much I practice to "get" something, and that I too needed to shift to just giving myself to practice and letting go of results.

Of course, there are some residents who come and go, or come regularly but don't seem to practice much in between. On very rare occasions someone is disruptive, or clearly just there to talk to someone from another yard. Buddhist practice isn't for everyone; only a small percent of prison city residents ever even check us out.

For me, I feel hugely privileged to be included in the prison city *sanghas*. I am endlessly inspired. I recently had some difficult family circumstances, and in the midst of it, I would think about particular residents and remember some of their sharing. The feeling of being connected to them personally, being supported by their practice, was very strong and very helpful. I felt held by our *sanghas*. If the residents of this painfully difficult city can find moments of equanimity, acceptance, and kindness to others in the midst of the punitive and violent city, surely I can too.

It has deepened my belief in our interconnectedness, our core humanity. Despite growing up in horrendous conditions, or immigrating to a racist country and being poorly treated, or making very poor choices, or being addicted, or some combination of these, people can choose to find liberation in the everyday of life. And I know that my liberation is intertwined with all beings, particularly the members of our prison city *sangha*.

Walt Opie:

You are not bringing God into the prison—he is already there!

—FATHER GEORGE WILLIAMS

When someone on the outside of this "terrible city" asks me what I've learned so far from going into prison, I tell them how it quickly becomes obvious that there are no "others" when you're inside prison, no "us" and "them," even though inmates are often discussed in those terms in our society. As I've heard the Dalai Lama say at several of his public talks, "We're all the same. Although we may have different skin colors, different clothes, different languages . . . we are basically all the same human beings."

In prison, one of the more obvious differences is the clothes people wear. State prisoners are required to wear thin, sky blue, prison-issue shirts and dark blue pants with "CDCR" stamped on them in yellow lettering. (CDCR stands for California Department of Corrections and Rehabilitation.) The right leg of each pair of pants has the word "PRISONER" printed in yellow down it in rather dramatic fashion. We outside visitors are not allowed to wear blue shirts or pants (including blue jeans) to differentiate us from the prison population "in case of emergency." I always wear a black t-shirt with a plaid shirt over it, and usually light brown pants.

Now that I've been going into the prison for a while, our different clothes don't really register in the same way. What matters is often much more personal. How is everyone doing? What has their week been like? Who in the group might be up for release soon? Has anybody suffered a loss in the immediate family? Did they practice meditation on their own this week at all? Right after meditation, we have regular check-in rounds where many of these questions get answered each week, which is always a highlight.

At first, not everyone tends to share what is really going on. Part of our job, as I've come to see it, is to create a safe space for each person to be vulnerable, or at least, more human than they can be out on the exercise yard or in their regular prison circumstances. This is how we slowly build a feeling of *sangha* (or community) in this often hostile or indifferent place. We sit in a circle in the rather bare-bones prison chapel surrounded by grey metal lockers with the names of many different religious groups written on them (one per faith): "Jewish, Nation of Islam, Wicca, Native Hawaiian, Seventh Day Adventist, Jehovah's Witnesses, Pagan, Rastafarian, Apostolic, Latter Day Saints, Catholic, Muslim . . . ." Each locker has a heavy padlock on it, but I believe one key fits them all. On the inside of the door to the Buddhist locker on Level II, someone has taped up the headline for a magazine article by Zen teacher Norman Fischer that says: "Life Is Tough—Six Ways to Deal with It." On the metal shelves of the locker are Buddhist books from many traditions, black zafus (meditation cushions), grey folded blankets, and singing bowls (bells). We even have a plastic Buddha statue that we put out on a piano bench covered in colored silk cloth during our *sangha* group.

When I first entered prison as a Buddhist volunteer a few years ago, I didn't know what the people I would meet inside might be like. The reality I've found is hard to put into words. Although many people do admit to ongoing issues with anger, I also hear many stories of generosity and kindness from those in our groups. They have even admonished me for assuming that generosity is rare in their city. "I share whatever I get from my family all the time," one guy said emphatically. Some of the residents we meet have been practicing Buddhism for decades. Two guys had even ordained as Buddhist monks while growing up in Cambodia or in a

Cambodian community in the US. One of those guys has since been released, and he said his reentry plan was to go live at a Buddhist monastery.

As I enter the prison, I sometimes think about how everyone has such a different perspective on being there. The Corrections Officers definitely have their point of view, which is all about security. Then there are the other people who work there—the medical staff, the food workers, the lawyers, and the volunteers like us. We all have our own perspectives. And then of course there are the inmates. They are required to be there. Most, if not all, would like to leave this city as soon as possible. Some of them are amazed that we volunteers are willing to come there at all. One resident asked me, "What motivates you to be here, when you could be doing so many other things?" I don't think I had a very satisfactory answer for him at the time. Today I would say, I go there to connect, to listen, and to share whatever I know. I might even say, as I think about it, that this is the best place I know for my own practice.

Speaking to a small group of us at his monastery outside Yangon, my Burmese teacher Sayadaw U Tejaniya said, "In daily life it's more obvious, the value of practice. Daily life has a lot of suffering, right? Without practice, we are finished." Then he laughed knowingly. This is magnified when I'm inside prison, surrounded by suffering. My faith in the power of practice comes alive. I've seen the relief many prisoners find when they really apply themselves to this practice of mindfulness and compassion.

One guy who came to our group on Level III often sat slightly away from the circle and rarely looked up to make eye contact. Yet he continued to show up week after week. Then he disappeared for well over a month. When he finally returned, something had changed. Now he wanted to speak during the check-in. It turned out that over a very short period of time, his beloved grandmother who raised him had died, and then he had been sent to solitary confinement for a fairly serious violation involving some contraband cell phones. During that dark time alone in "the hole," he remembered his meditation practice, following the breath. He said it worked in a way that nothing else ever had before. Now he is always there at our group, with his head held high and eyes ready to connect, one of our most enthusiastic *sangha* members. It was a remarkable turnaround.

My own spiritual practice is deeply informed by the teachings on lovingkindness and compassion, especially the *Metta Sutta*. One of the key sections states:

> *Even as a mother protects with her life*
> *Her child, her only child,*
> *So with a boundless heart*
> *Should one cherish all living beings:*
> *Radiating kindness over the entire world . . .*

I take this to mean we should literally cherish all living beings, especially fellow human beings. Given this, I feel nobody should be left out or written off, including the incarcerated members of our community. Of course, some people do need to be separated out from society in order to protect others as well as themselves. Yet I believe that everyone has the ability to learn from mistakes and reconnect with their hearts, unless they have some kind of severe mental condition that limits their ability to do so. This is taught in the *Angulimala Sutta* where a former serial killer becomes an enlightened monk under the guidance of the Buddha himself. So, everyone has this same potential for awakening and should be treated as such until they "remember who they really are," as Jack Kornfield often states. I also feel that the Buddha's teachings on generosity point to a spirit of service and selflessness, which leads us closer to our own liberation.

Generosity helps us feel more connected to others and reminds us that we live in a shared world.

One of my favorite teachings to share with the prison *sangha* members is contained in the *Dart Sutta*. In it, the Buddha talks about how when an "uninstructed worldling" is hit by a dart (or arrow), they often find themselves quickly being hit by a second dart, a mental one they have added through aversion to the pain. Then they "seek delight in sensual pleasure" as a way to escape the painful feelings. He even says this is because "the uninstructed worldling does not know of any escape from painful feeling *other* than sensual pleasure." As a recovering addict and alcoholic myself, I can really relate to this teaching, and many members of our prison *sangha* seem to as well. This is why we need a practice that can help us override our basic impulse to avoid pain by seeking distractions in the sense realm (my first impulse now is "ice cream" or "TV" but it used to be "rum"). The Buddha says that whenever an "instructed noble disciple" gets hit by a dart, he only experiences that first bodily dart, but he doesn't add the second mental one. "He harbors no aversion toward it." This is true peace, but it takes a strong mindfulness practice to overcome our habits and achieve this.

One weekend we held all-day practice sessions on two consecutive days for the two different Buddhist *sanghas* we meet with at the prison (on Security Levels II and III). Prior to the weekend session, I led our regular weekday services earlier the same week. One of the guys on Level II, a gentle, older African American man and lifer who is called Wolf (we've had three men in the same group who go by this nickname), pulled me aside to ask if I ever attend events at a certain Zen center. I said I had been there before, but was not active in that tradition. However, I told him I knew several members there. He asked if I could get a message to his old Zen teacher from when he was with a Zen Buddhist sitting group in another prison many years before. Then he said the name of his teacher—Myogen Steve Stücky.

I didn't know Myogen Steve Stücky personally, but I had followed the news of his diagnosis with late stage pancreatic cancer quite closely because he was diagnosed around the time my sister-in-law was diagnosed with the same condition. I realized that Wolf had not heard that his teacher had passed on. I then had to decide what to do in that moment. I broke the news as gently as I could that his teacher had died of cancer not long ago. Wolf seemed surprised but not overly emotional. I had followed the moving story of the courageous way this Zen teacher had faced his cancer right up until his death—with tremendous dignity and equanimity despite terrible bodily pain. As I recall, he had refused chemotherapy after just a few weeks due to the side effects.

Having been deeply moved by this encounter at the prison, I decided as part of my short *dharma* talk during the all-day practice session that I would include something about the death (and life) of this teacher. First, I spoke with Wolf at the start of the day. He said the news of his teacher's death had really affected him and he'd been sitting with it, and that he was glad to know about it even though it was painful news. I asked if he would mind if I mentioned him during my talk, and he said calmly, "Go ahead."

As part of my talk, I offered a quote from one of his teacher's very last public talks at the Zen center. Myogen Steve Stücky described a current practice he had where upon waking each morning he would sit up, place his hands together, and say the word "gratitude" to see what arose in his mind. "Whatever it is (that arises) is supporting me," he said. "And this life is completely beyond judgment or preference." He was still cultivating gratitude as he was dying of cancer.

I also read Myogen's Zen death poem, which includes the lines: *"This human body truly is the entire cosmos/ Each breath of mine, is equally one of yours, my darling."*

During the talk, I didn't see much emotion on Wolf's face, although I could tell he was paying close attention. What Wolf said later to me was that he and another guy who also knew Myogen agreed that I kind of reminded them of their old teacher, or at least that I looked like him to them both. I didn't think we looked much alike, but then I thought maybe it was just Wolf's way of saying he accepted his current circumstances with me in this role of prison *dharma* leader, even if I am not his old Zen teacher. For me, all of the teachings of the *dharma* were included in this exchange around his teacher. Everything is constantly changing, and that's not a problem when we face it squarely. We just refrain from adding that second mental dart when the painful stuff hits us.

Another time, while giving a *dharma* talk at the prison, I mentioned that my sister-in-law had recently passed away from pancreatic cancer. A few minutes later, one of the *sangha* members referred to the death of his mother several months before, which I knew about. He said his one regret was that he couldn't at least be there to see her at the end and to know how it felt to say goodbye in person. He wondered if he would have been attached to her body, even after she was gone. I said I was there when my father took his last breath, and I noticed that as soon as he was gone, I felt no more attachment to his body—something I hadn't expected. It was so clear to me at that moment, I said, that we really are not our bodies. This seemed to bring some comfort to the *sangha* member—at least some letting go. I was again reminded that we are all the same, and that often the best thing we as prison volunteers can offer is simply ourselves.

LEAVING THE BIG CITY AND FINDING HOPE IN THE BIG HOUSE

by Reverend Diane Wilde

A large number of inmates who come to Buddhist services in California's northern prisons are products of the street life in the city of Los Angeles. They are frequently Latino gang members known as Sureños, while black inmates are often affiliated with the Crips and Bloods street gangs. The Crips have a long and bitter rivalry with the Bloods, which continues once members are incarcerated.

Unfortunately, the intense rivalries and the politics in the gang lifestyle often intensify in the claustrophobic confines of prison. Instead of gangs "owning" various areas of the city of Los Angeles, they now "own" areas of the prison yard. Gang members self-segregate in this small prison city, with the tacit approval of custody staff. It is an unstated understanding that maintaining this segregation makes it easier for staff to maintain order. Leaving the gang lifestyle is notoriously difficult. Men who disavow their gang associates risk losing their lives. As men make that decision to abandon the gang moniker, they are quickly moved into Administrative Segregation ("the hole") or moved to another prison and designated as a "special needs" inmate. They will serve the remainder of their sentences under some sort of protective custody.

At Buddhist services, for the past five years, we have been slowly accepting rival gang members into our community. Habits are not easily abandoned and the men are initially wary of being in such close proximity with the "enemy." As inmates begin to understand the suffering they have caused themselves and others, they also develop the wisdom that clinging to a view of "us and them" will only cause more harm and unhappiness. It is an endless cycle of suffering. We encourage that the moral code of the city gang life be replaced by the Buddhist training in *"sila,"* or ethical behavior. *Sila* in prison is taught by way of the Five Training Precepts, the fourth of the Noble Eightfold Path:

1. Abstaining from killing or harming living beings: development of compassion and kindness
2. Abstaining from taking what is not freely given: development of generosity and non-attachment
3. Abstaining from sexual (and sensual) misconduct: development of restraint
4. Abstaining from lying: development of honesty and truthfulness
5. Abstaining from taking drugs or narcotics: development of health and mindfulness

Behind prison walls, they have a venue where they can be honest, vulnerable, and, for a short period of time, free.

> *All experience is preceded by mind,*
> *Led by mind,*
> *Made by mind.*
> *Speak or act with a corrupted mind,*
> *And suffering follows*

As the wagon wheel follows the hoof of the ox.
All experience is preceded by mind,
Led by mind,
Made by mind.
Speak or act with a peaceful mind,
And happiness follows
Like a never-departing shadow.

—*Dhammapada*

Virtuous conduct in the prison environment

It may seem an oxymoron to place the words "virtuous" and "prison" in the same sentence. Yet, that is what we practice: "virtuous behavior in prison." Prison is an amazing laboratory for investigating everyday behavior in an atmosphere that neither accepts nor, for the most part, rewards virtue. Inmates receive validation for their efforts, first from themselves, and secondly from the prison *sangha*. Occasionally there is support from staff who see beyond "knucklehead," which is frequently used when describing California inmates.

Inmates who come to Buddhist services are usually struck by the honest and pragmatic quality of the Five Training Precepts. These precepts are training of body, speech, and mind . . . truly an extraordinary and very challenging mindfulness practice. Prison *sangha* members are often confounded by how to incorporate these teachings in the brutal California prison setting. Their challenge is to find practical applications in their lives and thus discover the benefits for themselves. For many, this investigation of virtue becomes their primary mindfulness practice.

Sitting meditation in prison can be a challenge for many inmates. The reasons are many: the liberal dispersing of psychotropic drugs, the ever-present noise of clanging cell doors, the almost constant vociferous yelling and screaming, blaring music and TVs, the continual interruptions for "count" and being led to and from jobs and programs. And probably the biggest impediment to a regular meditation practice is the risk of practicing a behavior that other inmates and custody may find suspicious. Even the *vipassana* meditation suggestion of recognizing "sound as just sound" or "notice the feelings and reactions that come up from contact through the sense doors" is often too challenging. Unfortunately, in many cases, reaction to the prison environment often trumps meditation practice.

Due to these difficulties, the Five Training Precepts often become the main focus of inmate practice. These men would not be seen associating with each other "in the yard" due to prison politics. Prison politics are the standards prisoners have set for themselves, are tacitly supported by custody staff, and are viewed as a method for staying safe. Prison politics and who you associate with are based on gang affiliations, racial attitudes, and religious differences. Our prison *sanghas* are one of the few places where Latinos, blacks, whites, and "others" can sit and practice together. It is a place where vulnerability is not frowned upon, unlike in the yard, and it offers a respite from the rapacious prison setting.

Karma is also a topic that is much discussed in prison *sanghas*. We teach that karma is nothing more than cause and effect. The Buddha said it succinctly: *"Karma is intention . . . in thought, word, and deed."* In each moment, we have the freedom to make a decision about our own karma. This is why training with the Five Precepts is so important—it is this nexus of the present moment that determines much of our future.

At our service, we usually do a session of "mindful movement," once everyone has arrived. This is sometimes led by an inmate yogi, or an experienced volunteer. After twenty-five minutes of movement, we sit in meditation for thirty minutes. We have found that when the body is relaxed through movement, the mind tends to relax as well and the benefits of meditation are much more easily realized. A volunteer will often lead the meditation with some gentle guidance, such as: "First feel the body on the cushion or the chair, let thoughts and feelings come and go— just observe them without clinging. When the mind has settled, the instruction is to focus just on the breath and the breathing process."

After the meditation, we "check in" as a group. Sometimes the volunteer leader may have a question that each person answers after introducing themselves. One of my favorites is, "Tell us about an act of kindness you committed this week." This is practicing with the First Precept. After we have all had a chance to speak, we read our service with everyone taking part. Each of the Precepts is read and often the inmates will explain to the group how they practiced with them. Afterwards one of the senior volunteers will offer a "*dharma* talk," trying to leave plenty of time for discussion. We close with a dedication of merit, meaning we send out the hope that our good intentions will benefit all living beings everywhere.

Following are a few "insights" shared by inmate *sangha* members as they recounted their practice with the precepts. The last reflection is what took place during a daylong retreat when two rival gangs attended.

Compassion for "the enemy"

The evening's roundtable topic was, "What sort of kindness did you commit today?" Committing kindness in prison is, needless to say, frowned upon by both inmates and staff. It is a sign of weakness. Yet in our Buddhist *sangha*, we ask our members to take on this act of bravery and to notice how extending kindness resonates both in the mind and body. On this particular evening, all but one of our twenty inmate *sangha* members had performed a kind act that they were anxious to share with each other. (The inmate who said he hadn't done anything kind was quickly reminded that he had shared some of his "ramen" with a *sangha* member. Ramen is a form of currency in prison, and having packages of ramen offers a lot of leverage for "purchasing" other commodities, such as soap, toothpaste, and treats.) *Sangha* is one of the only places where compassion for others can be openly explored among people who do not associate with each other openly when they leave our group. "Dameon," a youngish looking, baby-faced, light-skinned, mixed-race inmate, took a big chance one morning when he practiced compassion for a custody staff person. Here's what he told us:

> *I work in the kitchen and we have to get there really early to prepare the meals for the day. So, there was a bunch of us showing up like at 3:30 a.m. For some reason, there was way more than we usually have and it was getting loud. The CO (custody officer) was trying to collect our IDs before we went into the kitchen. We had to line up and there wasn't much room to do that. There were so many of us that he was having trouble holding all the IDs. He started juggling them from one hand to another to keep them from falling. It was like he was shuffling cards. He couldn't hold them all, and all of a sudden, they popped out of his hands and were all over the floor. They were everywhere.*
>
> *Everyone started laughing and laughing. They were making nasty remarks and really enjoying watching him get so upset. He was so embarrassed and angry, I thought for sure he would have a heart attack. I've never seen a white guy so red! Something happened inside of me, and I felt bad for the guy. I never feel bad for the cops, but it just came over me. For some reason, I decided to help him pick up all the IDs. We were both down on the ground picking up the cards, just the two of us, and the other inmates were making fun of me now, but I didn't care. I felt bad for the guy. I've been laughed at and picked on and I know how*

it feels. It took a few minutes, and no one else helped, so we finished picking up the cards and all of us went into the kitchen where I was made fun of some more.

It was a bad morning. Everyone was asking, "Why'd you do that? He's a cop! That was so stupid!" I didn't say anything back, just did my kitchen job. A few hours later we lined up to leave. This is the time everyone tries to take some food back to their cells. They put it down their shirt fronts, in their waistbands, in their underwear . . . anywhere they can hide it. This same CO is patting everyone down as we walked past him and taking all the food that everyone was trying to take. I think he was really still mad about the cards, since usually they kind of look the other way when we take food. Not today. I hid some food in my clothes too, even though it was obvious it would be discovered. When it was my time to get patted down, he just looks at me full in the face and says, "You're good." Wow! Instant karma!

The whole *sangha* laughed and did high fives with Dameon. He exhibited exceptional bravery when he felt compassion—even more, for a CO—and followed it up with action, and we all loved the extraordinary response.

He said: *"I used to wear a wool coat, and all the lies and stupidity people would throw at me would stick. With this practice, I now wear a raincoat and everything slides off."*

"This assignment is stupid!"

At another maximum-security prison, the same assignment of "committing an act of kindness" was given. One man in particular, a small wiry Latino named Luis, rarely spoke in our group, maintaining a stubborn, seemingly irritated silence, but he faithfully came every week for years. He arrived early one evening, before anyone else had been released, and wanted to talk privately. He got right to the point, "I thought about you and your stupid assignment all week. Kindness! You have got to be kidding! I am a criminal! I killed a guy when I was a kid in front of my whole family! That was thirty-five years ago and I am never leaving here. I have life without parole. Kind? Well, I couldn't do it. The best I could do was be respectful. And I only did that because you'll have us sit in a circle and talk about being kind, and I knew I had to say something. So, all week I was respectful. I opened doors for people, stuff like that. I didn't smile, I just held doors open. I've never in the whole time I've been in prison given a shit about any of these idiots in here, so respectful for me is doing a lot!"

He stopped for a moment and continued slowly. "It's the first time I thought of other people. Opening the doors for these guys made me have to think about them. I didn't like it. I'm not someone who cares about other people. It can be dangerous in here. Then last week I got a letter. It is from my nephew. He wants to meet me. I've not heard from any of my family in thirty-five years. And he wants to get to know me!" With that, Luis began quietly crying, checking frequently to make sure no one had arrived and would see this raw display of emotion. He continued, "Do you think that was karma? I acted respectfully and things change like that? Does it happen that quickly?" I told him I had no idea, but I would like to think his new, kinder attitude may be spilling out in unforeseen ways. I had to hide my own tears.

Norteños (northerners) and Sureños (southerners) together at last!

On January 27, 2015, Buddhist Pathways Prison Project held our annual Silent Retreat Day at California State Prison, Sacramento, a Level IV prison. Most of the men were in for life and were considered dangerous. Per protocol, gangs are separated.

This daylong retreat was going to be unusual because we were told that we had to include members of Latino prison gangs called the Norteños (northerners) and Sureños (southerners). Northerners never attend Buddhist services because of the prison's segregation policy. Our prison *sangha* was only allowed to admit Latino members who are "Southerners." Southerners and Northerners do not mix . . . ever. That policy was now being called into question and we were one of the first programs asked to include both groups. Not only that, prison staff had an additional requirement. Because combining these two gangs was considered an "experiment in programming" and had potentially dangerous repercussions, the retreat would not be held in the sanctuary of the chapel. It would be held in the gym where armed security would be present at all times. We all knew that prison guards don't have a great deal of respect for Buddhist practice. During our services, they were known to hold boisterous conversations, ridicule the men, call out derogatory remarks, and repeatedly slam the large iron doors.

I told prison staff that we would agree to their mandate of including Northerners, but I had two requests of my own:

1. I requested that the Northerners be allowed to meet with the entire *sangha*, including the Southerners, the week before the retreat. I wanted the men to introduce themselves, and I wanted to teach some basic Buddhist concepts to the Northerners as well as conduct a practice meditation session and discussion together. Interestingly, this was approved by the yard captain.

2. On the day of the retreat, I requested that security guards limit loud conversations, not make derogatory remarks, and respect the atmosphere we hoped to create.

My requests were agreed to. We had a brief meeting with both groups a week prior to the retreat. I stressed that a *sangha* is a place of safety, we don't endanger each other, we practice listening respectfully to each other, and we withhold criticism or argumentative opinions. I asked the Northerners to consider that in one week we would be in silence for an entire day, all together. With that in mind, the safety and sanctity of *sangha* was a commitment everyone had to uphold. We then recited the Three Refuges together (I take refuge in the Buddha, the *Dharma*, and the *Sangha*) and sat in meditation for thirty minutes. It was surprisingly peaceful.

On January 27, Buddhist volunteers arrived. We brought food for a vegetarian lunch of sandwiches, fruit, bottled green tea, and cookies into the prison gym, a huge, frigid, dirty, disheartening room. Just imagine a giant gray box with peeling grayish-greenish paint, and a dusty cement floor etched with scratch marks from years serving as the overflow barracks for hundreds of inmates. Armed security were milling around . . . watching but also maintaining silence as we had requested. We chose the furthest corner of the gym as our practice area. Incense, flowers, three donated Buddhas, a candle, and our homemade altar cloth transformed that corner of the gym into a beautiful focal point for meditation.

Thirty men took part. Our teacher for the day gave a clear, practical *dharma* talk on the Four Noble Truths and the basics of practice. We then sat for thirty minutes. Afterwards, the teacher demonstrated walking meditation, with more sitting. Lunch was in silence and instructions on mindful eating as a meditation were given. *Sangha* members were encouraged to take at least thirty minutes to eat their meal.

As we were nearing the end of the day, our teacher brought the group back together at our meditation area and encouraged the inmates to talk about their experience of the day and encouraged any questions about practice. Comments and questions were far-ranging. One man said, "This felt normal and good and peaceful." Another man said this retreat laid out the path he sees he needs to follow. We stood up as a *sangha* and formed a huge circle, everyone holding hands. Thirty inmates and volunteers. We asked as we concluded the day that everyone introduce themselves to the group and describe briefly their experience of the day. Comments ranged from gratitude, to wonder, to commitment to the practice. The men helped us clean up, and at 3:30 pm, they were escorted back to their cells.

Later in the evening, when I went back for our regular Buddhist service, I asked the men this question, "What was the most difficult part of the day for you?" I expected to hear statements such as: "I was worried about my safety." "I couldn't stay with my breath." "I couldn't stop thinking." "I was in physical pain." These men said the most difficult part of the day was "Leaving." I didn't understand and asked for clarification. They answered, "The most difficult part of the day was leaving the retreat." They commented that for seven hours they were safe, authentic, and at peace. Gang affiliation, race . . . none of it mattered. They saw possibilities for themselves. Even in that grimy, gray gym with armed guards . . . they were free.

NOTES AND LINKS

*(Further information about people and concepts
mentioned in chapters or biographies.)*

Three Characteristics of All Phenomena. One place to begin the study of this
discourse is the access to insight website: Readings in Theravada Buddhism.
See, The Three Basic Facts of Existence. accesstoinsight.org.

  dukkha, suffering, unsatisfactoriness.

  anatta, no permanent self, emptiness.

  anicca, impermanence, change.

Three Pillars. The Buddha's teachings are composed of three segments: *sila*
(morality), *samadhi* (mental concentration), and *panna* (intuitive wisdom).
Note, The Eightfold Path.

Three Refuges. Three Jewels. Triple Gem.

  Buddha means "one who is awake." When we take refuge in the Buddha,
  we are remembering our own potential to liberate the mind.

  Dhamma (in Pali), *dharma* (in Sanskrit) has layers of meaning. Derived
  from the root "dhr," meaning to hold, support, it refers to 1) mental
  phenomena, such as ideas, memories, etc., 2) the natural or cosmic
  laws of the universe, 3) the wisdom teachings of the Buddha, and
  4) lawfulness, truth.

  Sangha refers not only to the community of ordained monks and nuns,
  but also to our local communities of *dharma* practitioners and to all
  those who are engaged in the work of awakening.

Four Brahmaviharas are "best abodes" or "dwelling places of the gods."

Metta is a quality of goodwill. *Metta* meditation is the cultivation of a steady, unconditional sense of connection that touches all beings without exception, including ourselves. The quality of *metta* is associated with three other qualities.

Karuna (Compassion) is our caring human response to suffering. A compassionate heart is non-judgmental and recognizes all suffering—our own and that of others—as deserving of tenderness.

Mudita (Sympathetic Joy) is the realization that others' happiness is inseparable from our own. We rejoice in the joy of others and are not threatened by another's success.

Upekkha (Equanimity) is the spacious stillness of mind, balance, that provides the ground for the boundless nature of the other three qualities. This radiant calm enables us to ride the waves of our experience without getting lost in our reactions. *See,* sharonsalzberg.com; and *Compassion and Emptiness in Early Buddhist Meditation,* by Bhikkhu Anālayo.

Four Foundations of Mindfulness. *Note,* Satipatthāna Sutta.

Form (*rupa-kaya*), which includes mindfulness meditations on the breath, the four postures, activities throughout the day, parts of the body, the four elements, and death meditations.

Feeling tones (*vedana*), which includes the noticing of pleasant/unpleasant/neutral sensations.

Heart/mind (*citta*), which includes the states of emotions and thoughts.

Mental qualities and analyses of experience (*dhammas*), which includes the teachings on the hindrances, the aggregates, the sense spheres, the awakening factors, and the Four Noble Truths. *See, Satipatthāna: The Direct Path to Realization,* by Anālayo; and *Mindfulness: A Practical Guide to Awakening,* by Joseph Goldstein.

Four Noble Truths.

> **The First Noble Truth**—There is *dukkha*, often translated as "suffering." Closer to "unreliable and stressful, unsatisfactory." *Dukkha* must be understood.
>
> **The Second Noble Truth**—Greed, hatred, and delusion are the basis of the cravings that cause suffering. The origination of *dukkha* must be abandoned.
>
> **The Third Noble Truth**—The cessation of *dukkha*. Having created the cause of suffering, we can abandon it. Its cessation must be realized.
>
> **The Fourth Noble Truth**—The way leading to the cessation of *dukkha*. The Eightfold Path. The path must be developed.

Four Postures, *Iriyapatha*. When walking, a bhikkhu knows "I am walking"; when standing, he knows "I am standing"; when sitting, he knows "I am sitting"; when lying down, he knows "I am lying down"; or he knows accordingly however his body is disposed."

Five Aggregates are patterns of identifying ourselves that arise and pass away: Form (*rupa*); Feeling (*vedana*); Perception, Cognition (*sanna*); Mental fashionings, Volition (*sankhara*); Consciousness (*vinnana*).

Five Contemplations.

> I am subject to old age; I am not exempt from old age.
>
> I am subject to illness; I am not exempt from illness.
>
> I am subject to death; I am not exempt from death.
>
> I must be parted and separated from everyone and everything dear and agreeable to me.
>
> I am the owner of my actions, the heir of my actions, I have my actions as my origin, as my relative, as my resort. Whatever actions I do, good or bad, of them I shall become heir.

Five Hindrances to be overcome and inhibited: Sensual desire (*kamacchanda*); Ill-will (*byapada*); Sloth and Drowsiness (*thinamiddha*); Restlessness and Worry (*uddhaccakukkucca*); Doubt (*vicikiccha*).

Five Precepts. At core, do no harm—protect life, take only what is freely given, do not exploit or manipulate others sexually or in any other way, be truthful and kind in speech, and abstain from intoxicants or other substances and experiences that poison the mind.

Six Sense Spheres. The awareness of knowing a sense object by means of a sense base: eye and visible forms; ear and sounds; nose and odors; tongue and flavors; body and tangible objects; mind and mental objects.

Seven Factors of Awakening to be developed for insight and wisdom: Mindfulness *(sati)*; Investigation *(dhammavicaya)*; Energy *(viriya)*; Rapture *(piti)*; Calm *(passaddhi)*; Concentration *(samadhi)*; Equanimity *(upekkha)*. *See, The Seven Factors of Awakening*—a series of talks given by Gil Fronsdal. audiodharma.org.

Eightfold Path. The path the Buddha taught for freedom from suffering:

Wisdom *(Panna)*—Right or **Wise Understanding** and **Intention.**

Ethical conduct *(Sila)*—Right or **Wise Action, Speech** and **Livelihood.**

Tranquility *(Samadhi)*—Right or **Wise Effort, Concentration** and **Mindfulness.**

Ten *Paramis* are the qualities necessary for liberation and enlightenment—the qualities of heart that spiritual seekers perfect over long lifetimes of practice, including this lifetime: Giving *(dana)*; Integrity *(sila)*; Renunciation *(nekkhamma)*; Wisdom *(panna)*; Energy *(viriya)*; Patience *(khanti)*; Truthfulness *(sacca)*; Resolve *(adhitthana)*; Kindness *(metta)*; Equanimity *(upekkha)*.

Access to Insight. Translations and readings in Theravadan Buddhism. *See,* https://www.accesstoinsight.org.

AN 8:54 and 5:58. *Anguttara Nikaya* consists of several thousand *suttas* arranged in eleven books *(nipatas)*.

Bhikkhu Analayo is a core faculty member at Barre Center for Buddhist Studies. *See,* buddhistinquiry.org/teacher/bhikkhu-analayo/

Anatta (not self). *Note,* Three Characteristics.

Anger. *See*, The Elimination of Anger: With two stories retold from the Buddhist texts, by Ven. K. Piyatissa Thera. accesstoinsight.org.

Anicca (Impermanence). *Note*, Three Characteristics.

Angulimala Sutta. See, Angulimala, A Murderer's Road to Sainthood, by Hellmuth Hecker. accesstoinsight.org.

Bahiya Sutta. See, Bahiya Sutta, translated by Thanissaro Bhikkhu; and *About Bahiya*, translated by John D. Ireland. accesstoinsight.org.

James Baraz started the Community Dharma Leader program, is a founding teacher of Spirit Rock Meditation Center, and creator of *Awakening Joy, 10 Steps to a Happier Life. See*, www.awakeningjoy.info

Bhikkhu is an ordained male monastic ("monk"); *Bhikkhuni* is a female monastic ("nun"). *Bikkhu* is also any practitioner of the teachings of the Buddha.

Bhikkhu Bodhi is president of the Buddhist Association of the United States and founder of Buddhist Global Relief. *See*, bodhimonastery.org.

Bodhisatta (in Pali), *Bodhisattva* (in Sanskrit) is a being who is on the path to being a Buddha, to being enlightened.

Tara Brach is founder of the Insight Meditation Community of Washington, DC (IMCW). *See*, tarabrach.com.

Eugene Cash is a core CDL 4 teacher and founding teacher of the San Francisco Insight Meditation Community. *See*, sfinsight.org.

Ajahn Chah is the venerated Thai forest monk whose students are instrumental in bringing Theravada to the west. *See*, ajahnchah.org.

The Charter for Compassion is a document that urges the peoples and religions of the world to embrace the core value of compassion. The charter currently is available in more than 30 languages and has been endorsed by more than two million individuals around the globe.

Dana is the Pali word translated as the practice of generosity. *Note,* Ten Paramis.

Dependent Origination. One place to begin the study of this discourse is *Maha-nidana Suta: The Great Causes Discourse*, translated by Thaissaro

Bikkhu. accesstoinsight.org; another is *The Great Discourse on Causation: The Mahanidana Sutta and its Commentaries*, by Bhikku Bodhi.

Dhammapada is a collection of the Buddha's teachings in verse.

Dharma (in Sanskrit) or **Dhamma** (in Pali). *Note,* Three Refuges.

Dharmagiri, which means sacred mountain, is a hermitage founded by Kittisaro and Thanissara on the border of Lesotho and South Africa. *See,* dharmagiri.org.

Dharma Seed. Dharma talks from Western Buddhist Vipassana teachers, freely offered by donation. *See,* dharmaseed.org.

Dukkha. *Note,* Three Characteristics.

Equanimity, *Upekkha*. *Note,* Brahmaviharas, Seven Factors of Awakening, and Ten Paramis.

Gil Fronsdal is the guiding teacher of the Insight Meditation Center (IMC) of Redwood City, where offerings include online dharma talks, instructions, and meditation timers. *See,* insightmeditationcenter.org; and audiodharma.org.

S. N. Goenka's technique of Vipassana meditation is taught at ten-day residential retreats throughout the world by donation, without fees. *See,* dhamma. org/goenka.

Joseph Goldstein is a cofounder of the Insight Meditation Society in Barre, Massachusetts, the Barre Center for Buddhist Studies, and the Forest Refuge. *See,* dharma.org/joseph-goldstein.

Trudy Goodman is founder and guiding teacher of InsightLA and guiding teacher and co-founder of the Institute for Meditation and Psychotherapy in Cambridge, Massachusetts. *See,* trudygoodman.com.

Homeless in Oakland. *Homeless 'War zone': Oakland Officials under Fire to Solve Crisis,* by Tammerlin Drummond. *See,* www.eastbaytimes.com, May 24, 2017.

Insight Dialogue was developed by Gregory Kramer. *See,* metta.org.

Jataka Tales. One source for the collection of some 550 anecdotes and fables depicting earlier incarnations—sometimes as an animal, sometimes as a human—of the being who would become Siddhartha Gautama is www.margostoryteller.net.

Jeffrey Jacob et al. (2009). Personal and Planetary well-being: Mindfulness meditation, pro-environmental behavior and personal quality of life in a survey from the social justice and ecological sustainability movement. *Social Indicators Research. Vol 93, No 2, 275-294.*

Jhanas. Meditative concentration. One place to start the study of *jhanas* is *The Experience of Samadhi, Richard Shankman*; another is *The Jhanas in Theravada Buddhist Meditation*, by Henepola Gunaratana. accesstoinsight.org.

Kamma or Karma. There are consequences for skillful/unskillful action. Consequences may be felt here and now, or in the next rebirth, or in some subsequent existence. In Majjhma Nikaya 136, the Buddha explains his Great Exposition of Kamma, in which he shows the minds of people are complex and they make many different kinds of kamma even in one lifetime, some of which may influence the last moment when kamma is made before death, which in turn is the basis for the next life. And Ajahn Sucitto says, "However, as some feedback doesn't occur immediately, and may even take years to occur, aspects of the feedback loop are chaotic." *Note*, Five Contemplations.

Karuna (**Compassion**). *Note*, Brahmaviharas.

Kilesa, Kleshas. Defilement are the unwholesome roots of Greed (*lobha*), Hatred (*dosa*), and Delusion (*moha*). *Note,* The Second Noble Truth.

Jack Kornfield is a co-founder of the Insight Meditation Society in Barre, Massachusetts and the Spirit Rock Center in Woodacre, California. *See,* jackkornfield.com/

Gregory Kramer is the founding teacher of Metta Programs and developed the practice of Insight Dialogue. *See,* metta.org/

Lama Surya Das is the founder of the Dzogchen Center in Cambridge, Massachusetts, and its branch centers around the country. *See,* dzogchen.org/

Dr. Lee Lipp graduated from the Community Dharma Leaders training and was a San Francisco Bay Area Buddhist meditation teacher in the traditions of Vipassana, Zen and Thich Nhat Hanh's Order of Interbeing. (1937–2016).

Audre Lorde, a black feminist lesbian, was an American poet, essayist and novelist, womanist, librarian, and civil rights activist and scholar (1934–1992). *Warrior Poet: A Biography of Audre Lorde*, by Alexis De Veaux.

Majjhima Nikaya. The Middle-Length Discourses consists of 152 discourses by the Buddha and his chief disciples, which together constitute a comprehensive body of teaching concerning all aspects of the Buddha's teachings. *See*, accesstoinsight.org.

MAP Qualitative Feedback. By Harrison Blum (2014). Mindfulness equity and Western Buddhism, by Harrison Blum reaching people of low socioeconomic status and people of color. *International Journal of Dharma Studies*. 2:10; and movingdharma.org/

Mara, the embodiment of desire, challenged the Buddha on the night of his enlightenment with every sensual desire. *See, The Demons of Defilement (Kilesa Mara)*, by Ajaan Lee Dhammadharo. accesstoinsight.org.

Meghiya. *Meghiya Sutta: Meghiya*, translated by John D. Ireland. accesstoinsight.org.

Metta. *Note*, Brahmaviharas.

Naropa **Institute** was begun by Chogyam Trungpa Rinpoche. *See*, www.naropa.edu.

New York City Street Tree Map. *See*, tree-map.nycgovparks.org.

New York Insight Meditation Center. *See*, nyimc.org.

Pali Canon. The oldest recorded literature of Buddhism in the Pali language (which is no longer spoken). Lessons and stories were memorized (and chanted) for over 400 years before they were written down in Sri Lanka in the Fourth Buddhist Council in 29 BCE.

Venerable Dr. Pannavati founded Heartwood Refuge Retreat Center. *See*, pannavati.org/

Parivāra **XII.2.** The Buddhist Monastic Code. *See, Vinaya Pitaka. The Basket of the Discipline*. accesstoinsight.org.

Saddha Sutta. (AN 5.38). *See, Saddha Sutta: Conviction*, translated by Thanissaro Bhikkhu. accesstoinsight.org.

Samadhi. The practice of mindfulness and concentration, which we use as a primary tool for investigating the teachings and examining the texture of experience directly. *Note,* Eightfold Path.

Sangha. *Note,* Refuges.

Sankhara (Pali); **Samskara** (Sanskrit). According to monk and scholar Bhikkhu Bodhi, the word *sankhara* has no exact parallel in English. It is translated as mental fabrications, proliferation, dispositions, volitional formations. Simply put, it is the mental process of concocting thoughts, labels, and perceptions into what we call thinking. It can also refer to the product of those thoughts.

Satipatthāna Sutta is the foundational text for the *Vipassana* Buddhist lineage that was written down in the Pali language from the memorized talks the Buddha gave during his lifetime (*sutra* is the Sanskrit and is used by other Buddhist lineages and for later teaching). The Buddha's instructions in the *sutta* would have the practitioner establish mindfulness through contemplation in four areas (*satipatthanas*). *Note,* Four Foundations; and *See, Satipatthāna: The Direct Path to Realization,* by Anālayo; and *Mindfulness: A Practical Guide to Awakening,* by Joseph Goldstein.

Sharon Salzberg is a cofounder of the Insight Meditation Society in Barre, Massachusetts. *See,* www.sharonsalzberg.com; and *Love Your Enemies: How to Break the Anger Habit,* by Sharon Salzberg and Robert Thurman. October 1, 2013.

Gina Sharpe is a core CDL 4 teacher, co-founder of New York Insight Meditation Center, and member of the Teachers Council at Spirit Rock Meditation Center. *See,* ginasharpe.org/

Gloria Taraniya Ambrosia. *See,* www.buddhistinquiry.org/teacher/gloria -taraniya-ambrosia/

Sila appears on many of the Buddhist lists. It is translated as virtue or morality and often is expressed as the Five Precepts. *Note,* Four Noble Truths, Paramis, and Eightfold Path.

SN 45.2. Samyutta Nikaya contains 2,889 suttas grouped or yoked together by a theme. *See, Samyutta Nikaya. The Grouped Discourses.* accesstoinsight.org/

Sri Nisargadatta Maharaj. *See, The Nectar of Immortality, Discourses on the Eternal,* edited by Robert Powell, PhD

Ajahn Sumedho is the founder of the Cittaviveka Forest Monastery in West Sussex and the Amaravati Buddhist Monastery in Hertfordshire. *See,* amaravati.org.

Sayadaw U Tejaniyā. *See,* ashintejaniya.org; and hear *dharma* talks at www .audiodharma.org/teacher/150

Thanissara is a CDL 4 core teacher and co-founder with Kitisarro of Dharmagiri, a hermitage in South Africa. *See,* www.dharmagiri.org

Thanissaro Bhikkhu, Ajaan Geoff, is abbot of Metta Forest Monastery, San Diego County, California, and translator and compiler of *dhamma* books and study guides, often available free of charge. *See,* accesstoinsight.org; and www.watmetta.org.

Theravadan lineage of Buddhists read and study the earliest collection of scriptures that were written down in the Pali language from the memorized talks the Buddha gave during his lifetime. Translated as "way of elders." *See,* accesstoinsight.org/theravada.html.

Thich Nhat Hanh is a spiritual leader, poet, and peace activist. *See, plumvillage.org;* and *Loosening the Knots of Anger Through Mindfulness.* Lion's Roar, April 24, 2017.

Vedana. Feelings/Feeling tones. *Note,* Four Foundations and Five Aggregates.

Vinaya is the monastic discipline, spanning six volumes in printed text, whose rules and traditions define every aspect of the bhikkhus' and bhikkhunis' way of life. *Note,* Parivāra.

Vipassana. Insight, understandings. *Note,* S.N. Goenka.

Carol Wilson. *See,* www.dharma.org/carol-wilson/

Larry Yang is a core CDL4 teacher, a core teacher and leader of the East Bay Meditation Center, and member of the Teachers Council at Spirit Rock Meditation Center. He is author of *Awakening Together: The Spiritual Practice of Inclusivity and Diversity. See,* www.larryyang.org.

ABOUT THE AUTHORS

ANGELA DEWS found the *dharma* in 1996 at Vallecitos Mountain Ranch in New Mexico on retreat from politics, journalism, and government, and began serious practice at Deer Park in California with Venerable Thich Nhat Hanh. She is certified as a Community Dharma Leader by the Spirit Rock and New York Insight Meditation Centers. She is also a graduate of the Dedicated Practioners training with Gina Sharpe and the Commit to Dharma program with Gina and Larry Yang. Angela mentors inmates through the Chuang Yen Monastery Prisoners Correspondence Course and co-leads the Buddha & Bill W *sangha* at New York Insight Meditation Center and the weekly Harlem Insight Sit.

MARGO MCLOUGHLIN is a writer, storyteller, and teacher, based in Victoria, British Columbia. She is graduate of the Harvard Divinity School and the Community Dharma Leader training program at Spirit Rock Meditation Center. For more than twenty years, she has been weaving storytelling into her work. She performs her own translations of the Jataka tales (stories of the Buddha's former lives) as well as world tales of generosity. Margo is the editor of two anthologies: *Seeds of Generosity: Storytelling in the Classroom*, and *The Giving Heart: Folktales for Exploring Generosity*.

SEBENE SELASSIE is a meditation teacher and certified Integral Coach®. She has been studying Buddhism since majoring in Comparative Religious Studies as an undergraduate at McGill University, Montreal. For over twenty years, she worked with children, youth, and families nationally and internationally for small and large not-for-profits. Her work has taken her everywhere from the Tenderloin in San Francisco to refugee camps in Guinea, West Africa. Sebene is a two-time breast cancer survivor.

GARY SINGER is a teacher at New York Insight Meditation Center and a graduate of the Community Dharma Leaders program. He has been practicing Vipassanna meditation since 1992 and integrates mindfulness into his psychotherapy practice. He is on the Guiding Teachers Council at NYI, and writes and gives workshops on mindfulness, work/life balance, and intercultural relationships.

HARRISON BLUM serves as the Buddhist Spiritual Advisor and Mindfulness Program Director at Northeastern University, Boston. He also works as a Staff Chaplain at Franciscan Children's hospital, where he teaches mindfulness meditation to adolescent patients on an acute psychiatric unit. He received a master of divinity, focused on Buddhist ministry, from Harvard Divinity School, and a master of education from Lesley University's Creative Arts in Learning Program. He's a board certified Chaplain and a Community Dharma Leader in the Insight Meditation tradition of Theravada Buddhism, and is particularly committed to increasing mindfulness equity—equal access to mindfulness training across potential barriers based on race or class.

ALEX HALEY is an assistant professor and the mindfulness program leader at the University of Minnesota's Earl E. Bakken Center for Spirituality and Healing, where he teaches, assists with research, and sets the strategy for the mindfulness program area. He has been trained by the Center for Mindfulness, the Somatic Experiencing Trauma Institute, Spirit Rock Meditation Center, the Insight Meditation Society, the Insight Meditation Center, and the Coaches Training Institute.

Carissa Jean Tobin is a Minneapolis-based teacher, writer, and coach. Her poem "Minneapolis at Large" was published in the 2014 Chinook Book. Her poem "The way we move" was published in The Talking Stick Vol. 26. Carissa's blog, "Good Work, Great Life," gives tips for simple living.

WILDECY DE FÁTIMA JURY has been practicing meditation since 2000. She graduated from the Dedicated Practitioner Program and the Community Dharma Leader program at Spirit Rock. In 2015, she received a non-monastic ordination through the Dharmacharya Program with the Venerables Pannavati and Pannadipa. She has taught at East Bay Meditation Center, where she is presently a visiting teacher. She has taught at LA Insight, at Sociedade Vipassana in Brasilia, and at Instituto Sattva in Anápolis, Brazil. She has studied different spiritual practices, including African and Native American. As a spiritual activist, she has worked with many multicultural communities and groups, including immigrants and refugees, LGBTQ women, youth, children, and marginalized men. She intends to remain active in creating *sanghas* that cultivate generosity, compassion, forgiveness, and unity. She is an artist, a writer, and a poet who is in the process of publishing in the United States and in Brazil.

EVE DECKER has been practicing Insight Meditation since 1991, and has taught groups, day-longs, and short retreats since 2006, particularly at Spirit Rock, the East Bay Meditation Center, and elsewhere in the Bay Area. She is a graduate of UC-Berkeley and of Spirit Rock's Path of Engagement and Community Dharma Leader training programs, and has been trained in the Hakomi approach to body-based psychotherapy. Eve is also a singer/songwriter and song leader who has, in groups and on CDs, combined the power of music and *dharma* practice, including the CD *IN: Chants of Mindfulness & Compassion.*

ALICE ALLDREDGE co-leads the Open-Door *Sangha*, a meditation group in Santa Barbara, California, where she teaches mindfulness/insight meditation and leads sitting groups at the University of California and in the local community. She has meditated for over twenty-five years and is a graduate of Spirit Rock's Community Dharma Leaders program. The same awe and curiosity that led her to explore the outer world through a career as a marine biologist and university science professor also led her to explore the even greater vastness of our inner world through meditation.

NAKAWE CUEBAS initially studied meditation in 1998 with Burmese meditation teacher Mr. Goenka, then began being mentored by Gina Sharpe in 2007. She has mentored inmates since 2010 through the Chuang Yen Monastery Prisoners Correspondence Course. Her present practice since 2013 is focused on long-term practice retreats, initially studying with Joseph Goldstein, among other teachers. nakawe is a midwife by profession, dedicated to bringing healthcare to poor communities, in particular among Latinas, and has worked for eleven years in a community healthcare center in the Bronx. nakawe is currently studying in the Insight Meditation Society Teacher Training program.

TRACY COCHRAN is editorial director of *Parabola* magazine. Her articles have appeared in *The New York Times, The Boston Globe, The Boston Review, O: The Oprah Magazine, New York Magazine, Publishers Weekly, Psychology Today,* and other publications. Her stories have been included in anthologies, including *The Best Spiritual Writing* series; *Writing for Their Lives*; and *Sacred Voices: Essential Women's Wisdom through the Ages.* In addition to working in publishing and in the film industry, she is certified as a Community Dharma Leader by the Spirit Rock Meditation Center, teaching mindfulness meditation and mindful writing retreats in the greater New York area.

BART VAN MELIK has been teaching personal meditation and Insight Dialogue since 2009, with a specific focus on working with diverse populations. He is a graduate of the Community Dharma Leaders program and is a graduate of the IMS/Spirit Rock Teacher Training program. His mentors include Joseph Goldstein, Carol Wilson, Gregory Kramer, and his son Lou. Bart teaches through the Metta Foundation and is a senior teacher at the Lineage Project. He also teaches meditation and yoga at a VA hospital, juvenile detention center, homeless shelters, and public schools in New York City. Bart holds an MA in Psychology of Culture and Religion from the

Nijmegen University in The Netherlands. His passion is supporting people to discover how they can find new ways to relate to the stress created by life circumstances.

JOSHUA BEE ALAFIA graduated from UC-Santa Cruz in 1995 with a BA in Theatre Arts/Film. He currently is a filmmaker and has worked as a teaching artist, teaching film, capoeira, tai chi, and mindfulness practice. He is a graduate of the Community Dharma Leaders program and lives in Chicago and New York.

DIANA GOULD has been a meditator for over thirty-five years, practicing Insight Meditation for twenty-three. She is a Senior Teacher at InsightLA in Santa Monica, where she leads sitting groups and offers classes. She has been a facilitator for the Vipassana Support Institute, and has taught meditation at the Learning Curve at the Gay and Lesbian Center. She is a graduate of the Community Dharma Leaders program at Spirit Rock, the Buddhist Chaplaincy Training Program at the Sati Center for Buddhist Studies, and the Teacher Training program with Trudy Goodman at InsightLA. She was awarded Volunteer of the Year in 2011 for her work with Vitas Hospice. As a television writer and producer, her credits include pilots, episodes, movies, and miniseries for network and cable. Her first novel, *Coldwater* (Rare Bird Books; 2013) was awarded Silver Medal for Best First Book (fiction) in the 2014 IBPA Benjaman Franklyn Book Awards, and was Book of the Year in the mystery category by *Foreword*.

 PAUL IRVING has practiced in Eastern and Western contemplative traditions for over forty years. He holds Spirit Rock Meditation Center's certification to teach in the community. Much of his teaching has been at San Francisco Insight, where he has also served as a board member and board president. At San Francisco Zen Center and Green Gulch Farm, Paul regularly co-teaches Transforming Depression and Anxiety, and Finding Ease, workshops developed by his late friend and mentor, Dr. Lee Lipp. Paul is also one of the facilitators for the weekly Transforming Depression and Anxiety practice class at San Francisco Zen Center. He currently works as a manager in the allied health field at UC-San Francisco, is a bike commuter, and lives in San Francisco's Mission district with his husband.

NANCY GLIMM has been practicing Vipassana meditation since 1996. She has been a part of New York Insight Meditation Center since its inception. Nancy is a 2012 graduate of the Community Dharma Leaders program. Her primary teacher is Gloria Taraniya Ambrosia. Nancy leads the Living Urban Dharma Monday Daytime Sit and Aging as a Spiritual Practice. She is a psychotherapist in private practice with over thirty-five years of experience. Her psychotherapy practice is informed by her spiritual practice.

ELLEN FURNARI is a graduate of the Community Dharma Leaders program at Spirit Rock and teaches Buddhism in prisons. She shares the *dharma*, perhaps more widely than some would like, wherever she goes. Ellen is a consultant and researcher with a particular focus on unarmed civilian protection/peacekeeping, and recently wrote for and edited a volume titled "Wielding Nonviolence in the Midst of Violence: Case Studies of Good Practices in Unarmed Civilian Protection." She is the mother of two wonderful and beautiful grown daughters and recently became a grandmother.

NOBANTU MPOTULO is a teacher and co-director of Dharmagiri Sacred Mountain Retreat, KwaZulu Natal, South Africa. She is a qualified mentor and coach, an Investors-in-People prac-tioner, and a trainer. She is a certified Neruo-Linguistic Programming (NLP) practioner and a meditation teacher. In the 1990s, Nobantu was a co-facilitator of the Truth and Reconciliation Work-shops for both victims and perpetrators of violence in South Africa. She facili-tates Leadership Development Workshops for UN Peacekeeping managers and leaders, focusing on managing and leading with courage through the stressful situations. She also facilitates and leads self-care modules for USAID leaders based in challenging countries. She finds amazing benefits in integrating Mindfulness in leadership development.

JD DOYLE is a core teacher at the East Bay Meditation Center and one of the founders of the Alphabet *Sangha*. They've completed the Community Dharma Leader Program, the Dedicated Practitioner Program, and are currently in the Spirit Rock Teacher Training program. They are committed to celebrating the diversity of our human *sangha*, expanding concepts of gender, and living in ways that honor the sacredness of the earth.

RACHEL LEWIS has spent over 350 nights on silent retreat since 2003. She has taught many classes on the Buddhist lists since 2010. Her paid work at the University of British Columbia in Vancouver is only barely related to her physics PhD.

ROSEMARY BLAKE has been meditating for more than thirty years. After a career as an executive in the health care and retirement financial services industries, she graduated from the Community Dharma Leaders training and began teaching insight meditation at New York Insight Meditation Center. She attends at least one monthlong residential Vipassana retreat every year as a way to deepen her practice. She is also former president of the board of Insight Meditation Society in Barre, Massachusettes.

PAMELA AYO YETUNDE is Assistant Professor of Pastoral and Spiritual Care and Counseling at United Theological Seminary of the Twin Cities. She came to United in 2017. She received her ThD from Columbia Theological Seminary in Decatur, Georgia, where she specialized in pastoral counseling. Her research and scholarship focus on Object Relations Theory and psychotherapy, Buddhist psychology, Womanist Theology, Christian-Buddhist spiritual transitional stages, Black lesbian poet Audre Lorde as a spiritual and psychological resource, and chaplain formation. Yetunde has published a number of blog and magazine articles and has written journal articles, as well. Yetunde lives in Minnesota with her spouse. She is an interfaith Buddhist practitioner.

TUERE SALA is a Guiding Teacher at Seattle Insight Meditation Society and the founding teacher of the Capitol Hill Meditation Group. She is a retired prosecuting attorney who has practiced Vipassana meditation for over twenty-five years. Tuere believes that urban meditation is the foundation for today's practitioner's path to liberation. She has a long history of assisting others in establishing and maintaining a daily practice, including practitioners living with high stress, or past trauma, and those who have difficulty sitting still. She is inspired by bringing the *Dharma* to nontraditional places.

WALT OPIE is a volunteer prison *dharma* leader and the Executive Director of Buddhist Pathways Prison Project, which serves prisons across the state of California. He is a graduate of the Spirit Rock Community Dharma Leaders program and the Sati Center Buddhist Chaplaincy program. For the past six years, Walt has led the Berkeley Dharma and Recovery meditation group. He has an MFA in Writing from California College of the Arts.

DIANE WILDE has studied meditation in various traditions since 1990. In 2001, she was a founding member of Sacramento Insight Meditation Center, where she co-teaches. She founded and is a board member of the Buddhist Pathways Prison Project (BP3). At BP3, she is a volunteer chaplain along with seventy-five other volunteers who offer Buddhist services at numerous California prisons and jails. She is a graduate of Sati Center's Buddhist Chaplaincy program and Spirit Rock Meditation Center's Community Dharma Leadership training program. She is a board member of Sati Center for Buddhist Studies and of Sacramento Dharma Center. In 2015, she was lay-ordained at Insight Meditation Center as a Buddhist minister by her teacher Gil Fonsdahl.

INDEX

Heartwood Refuge Retreat Center,
186
heights, 130
Hillside International Truth Center,
169
Holistic Life Foundation, 22
homelessness, 139
honesty, 85, 212
hopefulness, 176
hopelessness, 31, 40
housing, 173–174
Howard University, 170–171
humility, 16
hungry ghosts, 113–114, 198
hurrying, 43
hyper-connectedness, 27

identity, 14–15
Ignatius House, 169
illness, 43
immigrants, 30, 84
imperfection, 51, 53
impermanence, 6–7, 60–61, 71, 73,
97, 161, 179
Impermanence (Cochran), 75–79
inadequacy, 48
incarceration. *See* prison
indigenous peoples, 30
injustice, 140, 141
insight, 79
Insight Dialogue, 187
Insight Meditation, 20, 173
Insight Meditation Society (IMS),
20–21, 24
inspiration, 88
instability, 180
integrity, 145
interaction, 143

interfaith, 165–174
Interfaith Community Initiatives,
172
International Symposium for
Contemplative Studies, 20
intolerance, 188
intoxicants, 199
invitations, 25
iriyapatha (four postures), 35
Irving, Paul, 103–109
isolation, awareness and, 15

Jackson, Milt, 73
Jataka tales, xviii
jealousy, 188
jhanas (meditative states or
absorption), 41
Johnson, Mordecai Wyatt, 166, 170–
171, 174
Jones, Marlene, 40
Jones Beach, 73
joy, 100, 141, 173
judgement, xvii, 14–16, 157, 185
juvenile detention centers, 86

kalyanamittas (spiritual friendships),
38
karma, 43, 99, 214, 218
karuna (joy), 100, 101, 141
Kashi Atlanta Urban Yoga Ashram,
169
kaya (body), xix
Kehilla Community Synagogue, 47
khanti (patience), 147–148
kickboxing, 121–124
Kickboxing with the Dharma (Furnari), 121–124
kilesas (defilements), 41